Excel

ADVANCED SKILLS

ENGLISH

YEAR 5

AGES 10–11

GRAMMAR AND PUNCTUATION WORKBOOK

Get the Results You Want!

PASCAL PRESS

Laura Anderson

Reprinted 2015, 2016, 2018, 2019, 2020, 2021, 2022, 2025

ISBN 978 1 74125 401 3

Pascal Press
PO Box 250
Glebe NSW 2037
www.pascalpress.com.au

Publisher: Vivienne Joannou
Project editors: Mark Dixon and Leanne Poll
Edited by Leanne Howard
Reviewed by Dale Little and Kristine Brown
Cover and page design by DiZign Pty Ltd
Typeset by lj Design (Julianne Billington)
Printed by Vivar Printing/Green Giant Press

Contents

To the student

This book explains the rules of grammar and punctuation that you need for Year 5.

Each unit focuses on two or more grammar rules. Before each rule is explained, there is a text that lets you see how the rule works in everyday writing. These texts are important as they are models of the different text types and will help you in your own writing. At the end of each unit there is also a short NAPLAN-style test that lets you see how well you have understood the grammar rules.

Most of the activities can be written in this book, but you will have to use your own paper for the writing activity at the end of each unit. I suggest you buy a notebook or folder for this. The writing activities are very important. The more you do, the faster your English will improve. If you are not sure how to write something, use the example texts as a model.

It is important that you work through this book from Unit 1 to the end. This will help you build your skills and become a more confident speaker and writer of English. Make sure that you understand the work in each unit before you go on to the next one. Remember to have a dictionary handy as you work through the book, and to ask for help if you need it. There is a glossary on pages 109–110 that explains the grammatical terms used in the units.

I hope you enjoy reading the texts and doing all the activities.

Good luck!

Laura Anderson

About this book

This book consists of eighteen units, each covering one or more aspects of grammar or punctuation. Each unit is theme-based and contains two texts designed to introduce the grammatical features and to show students how they function in context. These are followed by detailed explanations of how and why the grammar features are used, as well as exercises that allow students to put the knowledge they have acquired into practice. As an aid to revision, there is a glossary at the end of the book that summarises the grammatical terms used in the units.

The exercises in the units are organised as follows:

Let's find them!

- These exercises require students to find examples of the grammatical feature in question in the texts. They are straightforward exercises designed to test recall.

Let's go to the next step!

- This set of exercises is more difficult, requiring students to apply the knowledge they have acquired.

Let's aim high now!

- These are challenging exercises, again requiring students to apply what they have learnt.

Let's put it all together now!

- This is an editing exercise designed to test the students' understanding of the material covered in the whole unit. It also acts as a revision exercise.

Let's have fun!

- Although this exercise is designed to be fun, it is also challenging. It reinforces the material learnt.

Let's have a test!

- This series of eight NAPLAN-style questions helps students revise for the NAPLAN Tests and also tests their knowledge of the material learnt in the unit as a whole. The questions are graded so that they increase in difficulty.

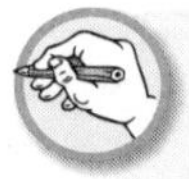

Let's write now!

- This activity encourages students to write their own text in which they use the grammar and punctuation they have learnt in the unit. The texts are based on the theme and text types featured in the unit.

Most of the exercises in this book consist of seven questions, as we believe they give students the practice they need to fully grasp the rules of grammar and punctuation.

Unit 1 Celebrating New Year

Focus

Nouns; capital letters

New Year traditions

Although people in many **countries** around the **world** bring in the New Year with fireworks displays, each **country** has its own New Year traditions. A brave **Roman**, for example, might celebrate the arrival of the New Year by diving off the Cavour Bridge into the Tiber River. The Dutch also take to the **water** on New Year's Day, when many of them can be seen dashing into the icy North Sea in swimming costumes and orange hats.

To bring them good luck in the coming year, people in the Philippines buy round fruit such as grapes on **New Year's Eve**. Fruit is also part of the New Year celebrations in Mexico, where people eat twelve grapes as the clock strikes midnight. Each time they swallow a grape, they make a wish.

One of the most common New Year traditions is to make resolutions for the coming year, such as deciding to exercise more or to eat a healthier diet; however, research shows that most people break their New Year resolutions before the end of **January**!

by Jamal

This is a **report**. Jamal uses **common** and **proper nouns** to name particular people, places, animals and things in his report on New Year traditions around the world.

Nouns
- are the names of animals, places, things, people and events; for example, **world**, **Roman**.
- can be singular or plural; for example, **country → countries**.

Common nouns are the general names of people, animals, places, things and events; for example, **water**.

Proper nouns
- are the particular names of people, animals, places, things or events; for example, **New Year's Eve**.
- always start with a **capital letter**.
- include the names of the days of the week and the months of the year; for example, **January**.

Rule! If the particular name of a person, animal, place or thing has more than one word in it, all of the words start with a capital letter; for example, **New Year's Eve**.

Let's find them!

Find these **common** and **proper nouns** in the text. Remember to start the proper nouns with a **capital letter**!

1. a bridge ______________________
2. a river ______________________
3. the people who swim in the North Sea ______________________
4. things that are orange ______________________
5. a country ______________________
6. a type of fruit ______________________
7. something that shows us what time it is ______________________

Let's go to the next step!

Underline the **common nouns** and circle the **proper nouns** in these sentences. For example: I celebrated New Year's Eve in Melbourne with my friends.

1. In Scotland, New Year is called Hogmanay.
2. Gran always bakes a special cake on New Year's Day.
3. Mum and Dad are going to bring in the New Year in the city.
4. We always bring our dog indoors before the fireworks go off.
5. My teacher, Mr Jones, will be in Singapore on December 31st.
6. We went to their house on Christmas Day and they visited us on New Year's Eve.
7. In some countries in Asia, New Year is sometimes celebrated as late as February.

Let's aim high now!

Show which words in these sentences are **proper nouns** by giving them **capital letters**.

1. Last year we celebrated chinese new year in shanghai. ______________________
2. In some cultures, the first day of the new year is celebrated in march. ______________________
3. There is always a party at the sydney opera house on new year's eve. ______________________
4. The jewish new year is called rosh hashanah and is celebrated in september. ______________________
5. On the stroke of midnight, colourful fireworks burst from the eiffel tower in paris. ______________________
6. Places like auckland, hong kong, beijing and sydney are among the first to bring in the new year. ______________________
7. My little brother, tom, has finally worked out that christmas is exactly seven days before new year. ______________________

From: Sammy Smith
Subject: Happy New Year!
Date: 2nd January
To: Charlie Lloyd <challoyd@firstnet.com.au>

Hi Charlie,

Happy New Year! I hope we all have a great year in Year 5.

We are still in New York. We brought in the New Year at Times Square with **hordes** of other people. It was a huge celebration! Mum said she could actually feel the **energy** in the crowd. We had a good view of the entertainment on the stage, and we watched some very big stars performing, like One Direction! Then just before midnight they started lowering the Times Square Ball, which sparkles because it's covered in a heap of crystals. There was a humongous cheer when the clock struck midnight, and everyone was hugging and kissing each other. I got hugged by some complete strangers!

We've met a family from Australia and are having lunch with them tomorrow. The girl, Lisa, is my age. She also likes to have fun!

I can't wait to show you the great present I've bought you. I'll call you as soon as I get back next week. See you then.

Hugs and kisses,
Sammy

This is an **email**. An email is a way of communicating with others. Sammy uses **collective nouns** to name groups of people and things and **abstract nouns** to name things we cannot see or touch while telling her friend, Charlie, about things she has seen and experienced in New York.

Collective nouns are the names of groups of people, animals, places and things; for example, **hordes**.

Abstract nouns are the names of things we cannot see or touch; for example, **energy**.

Let's find them!

Tip!
Abstract nouns are often feelings or qualities; for example, **confusion**, **bravery**.

Find these **collective** and **abstract nouns** in the text.
Write the name of the group of

1. people who gave off a lot of energy ______________________
2. crystals that cover the ball ______________________
3. people from Australia ______________________

Write the name of something that

4. was huge ______________________
5. was happening on the stage ______________________

6. was humongous ____________________

7. Lisa likes to have ____________________

Let's go to the next step!

Complete these sentences by filling in a **collective** or **abstract noun** from the box. Write down what type of noun it is in the space next to the sentence.
For example: People gasped in awe as the fireworks lit up the sky. abstract noun

band	terror	bouquet	excitement	festivities	wardrobe	set

1. The celebrations caused great ____________ in the city. ____________
2. We were given a ____________ of rules to follow on New Year's Eve. ____________
3. Some animals run away in ____________ when the fireworks start. ____________
4. She has a ____________ of clothes from which to choose an outfit. ____________
5. They asked the winning ____________ to play the last song of the night. ____________
6. Mum is always happy when the Christmas and New Year ____________ are over. ____________
7. Just before midnight, they presented the entertainer with a ____________ of flowers. ____________

Let's aim high now!

Underline the **collective nouns** and circle the **abstract nouns** in these sentences.
For example: The gang of boys waited in silence for the entertainment to begin.

1. He found information about New Year traditions in the library.
2. The guests of honour arrived at the celebration in a fleet of cars.
3. A galaxy of lights lit up the darkness as the clock struck midnight.
4. I was telling the truth when I said that the orchestra was outstanding.
5. I thought that the troupe of dancers from Brisbane gave the best performance.
6. People were grouped in clusters, waiting to hear the mayor's New Year message.
7. Imagine my amazement when I discovered that I could buy a whole box of fireworks!

Let's put it together now!

This student has written some of these **nouns** from reports about New Year celebrations in the wrong columns. Put a cross next to the ones that are in the wrong place and rewrite them under the correct heading.

Common nouns	Proper nouns	Collective nouns	Abstract nouns	Plural nouns
singer	audience	mob	mosquitoes	fireworks
stage	Eiffel Tower	staff	microphone	bodies
building	New Year's Eve	team	applause	joy
costume	children	London	happiness	Lady Gaga
fun	Beijing	orchestra	fright	knives

Let's have fun!

On December 31st or January 1st, depending on where they live, millions of television viewers around the world watch Sydney bring in the New Year with its famous fireworks display on the harbour.

Name the people, places, animals and things in this picture of Sydney celebrating New Year by filling in an appropriate noun from the box next to each number. Write the **common nouns** in black, the **proper nouns** in red, the **collective nouns** in blue and the **abstract nouns** in green. The first one has been done for you.

bunch
laughter
Sydney Harbour Bridge
fish
astonishment
Mandy
boat
Nick

1 flock

2 ____________________

3 ____________________

4 ____________________

5 ____________________

6 ____________________

7 ____________________

8 ____________________

9 ____________________

Let's have a test!

1 Choose the sentence in which the nouns have been written correctly.

- ○ We spent New Year's eve in London.
- ○ We spent new year's eve in London.
- ○ We spent New Year's Eve in London.
- ○ We spent New Year's Eve in london.

2 Choose the sentence in which the nouns have been written **incorrectly**.

- ○ The Jacksons went to Thailand for Christmas and New Year.
- ○ The Jacksons always bring in the new year in Thailand.
- ○ The Jacksons may not spend new year in thailand next year.

> **Tip!** Shade the circle with the correct answer

3 Choose the noun that completes this sentence correctly.

A ______________ of rain threatened to spoil the New Year's Day celebrations.

- ○ pile
- ○ shower
- ○ procession
- ○ group

4 Choose the list of abstract nouns.

- ○ curiosity, resolution, tradition, joy
- ○ fireworks, grapes, barges, clocks
- ○ choir, pack, convoy, assortment
- ○ Darwin, Perth, Adelaide, Melbourne

5 Which sentence does **not** contain a plural noun?

- ○ The children watched the fireworks display on television.
- ○ The man and woman got home late on New Year's Day.
- ○ The people enjoyed the fireworks display.

In questions 6–7, choose the word that completes the sentence correctly.

6 There was great ______________ in the decorations at New Year.

- ○ vary
- ○ varies
- ○ variety
- ○ varieties

7 The Mayor showed her ______________ by presenting the organisers with medals.

- ○ thanked
- ○ thanks
- ○ thanking
- ○ thank you

8 Which word does **not** complete this sentence correctly?

Some New Year ______________ are more unusual than others.

- ○ celebrations
- ○ festivity
- ○ traditions
- ○ rituals

Let's write now!

Answer one of the following.

1. Find out about a culture that celebrates New Year differently from you by looking in books or on the Internet. Write a **report** on what you have found out.
2. Write an **email** to one of your friends and tell him or her how you or your family brought in the New Year this year.

Try to use a mixture of **common**, **proper**, **collective** and **abstract nouns** in your report or email.

Unit 2 Money

Focus

Pronouns

Money doesn't grow on trees

If **he** was going to get that new bike before the big race, he would have to earn some money to help pay for it. As Mum liked to remind him, money doesn't grow on trees. Mum had agreed to give him an advance on his birthday money, and he had managed to save some of his pocket money, but it still wouldn't be enough.

Simon tried to convince **himself** that there were lots of ways a smart 11-year-old could earn money. He could wash cars, walk dogs, babysit the neighbours' children … that's when he realised that it wasn't going to be easy. **Which** neighbours would allow him to look after their children? Whose dogs would he take for a walk? His neighbours might let him wash their cars, but would there be enough of them to make it worth his while? They might not even pay him that well. No! He would have to think of a better idea. Then it struck him! There were lots of things Grandma could no longer do for herself—like getting things down from the tops of cupboards (she said it made her dizzy). Well, he would offer to help Grandma—at a price.

This is part of a **narrative**. A narrative tells a story. The author uses **personal pronouns** in place of nouns to avoid repeating them, **reflexive pronouns** to refer back to nouns and other pronouns, and **interrogative pronouns** to ask questions while telling how Simon planned to earn more money.

Personal pronouns are used in place of common and proper nouns to avoid repeating the nouns all the time; for example, **he** is used in place of Simon.

Reflexive pronouns

- refer back to a common or proper noun or another pronoun; for example, **himself** refers back to Simon.
- always end in *self* or *selves*.

Interrogative pronouns ask questions; for example, **Which?**

The other interrogative pronouns are Who?, Whom?, Whose? and What?

Let's find them!

Underline all the **personal**, **reflexive** and **interrogative pronouns** in the text, and then choose eight of them to write in the spaces on the following page. Don't use the ones in bold.

Use the lists of pronouns on this page to help you find the words in the text.

Tip!

Personal and **reflexive pronouns** can be:

Singular—I, me, myself; you, yourself; he, him, she, her, it, himself, herself, itself.

Plural—we, us, ourselves; you, yourselves; they, them, themselves.

1 ______________________
2 ______________________
3 ______________________
4 ______________________
5 ______________________
6 ______________________
7 ______________________
8 ______________________

Let's go to the next step!

In the following sentences, underline the **personal pronouns**, draw a circle around the **reflexive pronouns** and put a box around the **interrogative pronouns**.

For example: [Who] will tell _them_ that _they_ have to earn the money (themselves)?

1. What do they plan to do with all that money?
2. Which of these games are you going to buy?
3. The man said he would use the money to build himself a new house.
4. Mum said she would join me after she had withdrawn money from the ATM.
5. I won't be able to afford the new skateboard unless you lend me some money.
6. I said I would give them an extra five dollars if they helped me clean the garage.
7. He told us that we would be helping ourselves in the future if we started saving money now.

Let's aim high now!

Complete the following sentences with a **pronoun** from the box. At the end of each sentence, write down whether the pronoun you have chosen is a **personal pronoun**, a **reflexive pronoun** or an **interrogative pronoun**.

For example: Share the money with _them_. personal pronoun

it	Whose	themselves	I	Who	herself	me

1. "__________ ten dollar note is this?" asked the man. __________
2. I asked her to buy __________ a new wallet for my birthday. __________
3. I bought a chocolate bar and gave __________ to the little boy. __________
4. __________ think it's a great pity that money doesn't grow on trees! __________
5. "__________ is going to help me count these coins?" asked Dad. __________
6. I said I would give them each a dollar if they behaved __________. __________
7. She helped __________ to another muffin, even though she hadn't paid for it. __________

Money doesn't grow on trees

That afternoon, when Simon had finished **his** homework, he rushed down to Grandma's cottage at the bottom of their garden. She immediately offered him some of her freshly baked scones with jam and cream.

Between mouthfuls, Simon asked casually, "Grandma, do you need help with anything?" He was overjoyed when she said yes, but he wasn't prepared for what it was she wanted him to do ... wash and style her hair!

"My old arms are getting too stiff to do it myself," she said, "and going to the hairdresser is expensive." She offered to pay him $10 a week and said he could start straight away.

"You'll need **this**," she said, handing him the shampoo, "and these." She handed Simon a box of sausage-shaped objects. She said they were rollers.

"Hold a section of my hair in your hand like this," she said, demonstrating, "then twist it around the roller and pin it in place. Your fingers aren't as stiff as mine, so you'll be able to do it much faster." Simon wasn't so sure about that! "And don't worry," Grandma added, "I won't tell anyone. This will be our little secret."

This is another part of the **narrative**. The author uses **possessive pronouns** to show ownership and **demonstrative pronouns** to point out specific nouns while telling how Simon and Grandma helped each other.

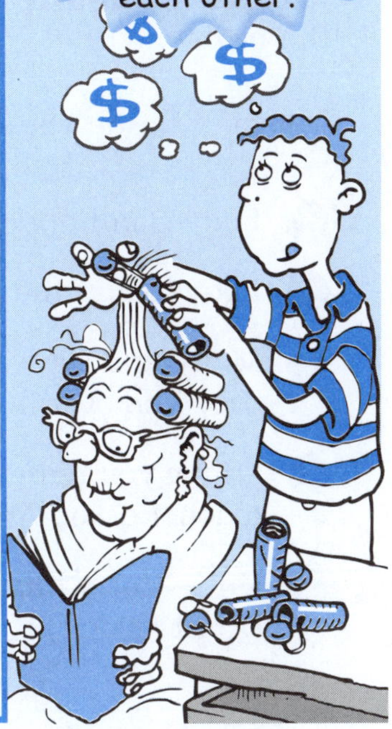

Possessive pronouns

- are used in place of common and proper nouns to avoid repeating the nouns; for example, **his** in place of Simon.
- show ownership, or possession; for example, **his** shows that the homework belongs to Simon.
- can be singular or plural.

Singular	Plural
my, mine	our, ours
your, yours	your, yours
his, her, hers, its	their, theirs

Demonstrative pronouns are sometimes used to point out specific nouns; for example, **this** is used to point out the noun *shampoo*.

Let's find them!

Underline all the **possessive** and **demonstrative pronouns** in the text and choose seven of them to write in the spaces. Don't use the ones in bold.

Tip! There are four demonstrative pronouns: **this**, **that**, **these** and **those**.

1 ______________________

2 ______________________

3 ______________________ 6 ______________________

4 ______________________ 7 ______________________

5 ______________________

Let's go to the next step!

Replace the **nouns** in brackets with a **possessive** or **demonstrative pronoun** from the box.

their	those	your	his	hers	her	this

1. I gave Grandpa (Grandpa's) ____________ wallet.
2. I gave Mum the money to deposit in (Mum's) ____________ bank account.
3. Molly and Jess counted all (Molly and Jess's) ____________ coins and discovered they had over fifty dollars.
4. "Have you remembered to bring (Andy's) ____________ gold coin donation?" the teacher asked Andy.
5. Uncle Harry has a lot of money in his savings account, but Aunt Hilda has more in (Aunt Hilda's) ____________.
6. "____________ (hundred dollar note) belongs to me," said Billy's uncle, putting the hundred dollar note in his pocket.
7. "I know these bananas are cheaper, but I'd rather have (bananas) ____________," said Pam, pointing to the more expensive bananas.

Let's aim high now!

Complete these sentences with a **possessive** or **demonstrative pronoun** from the box. Use each word once.

his	yours	your	hers	my	that	these	this	mine	its

1. This is my share of the money and ____________ is ____________.
2. After he paid me, I handed the mouse over to ____________ new owner.
3. The farmer earns ____________ keep by selling the wool from the sheep.
4. My reward for helping Dad clean up the yard was bigger than ____________.
5. "__________ are __________ coins," said the girl, pointing to a pile on the table.
6. "I found this $20 note, so it's __________," said Joanne, holding on to it tightly.
7. "How much of __________ hard-earned cash did you spend on __________?" asked Dad, pointing to his nephew's new car.

Let's put it together now!

This student has written some of the **pronouns** in this part of her narrative incorrectly. Underline the ones that are wrong, and write them correctly in the spaces below.

The day of the race finally arrived. Simon checked he's bike again, then placed it carefully on the rack behind they car. Simon was proud of heself because he had found the extra money to pay for the bike. But he knew that if it hadn't been for Grandma, he wouldn't have been able to do it. He looked at hers now and she winked at him. She pointed to her hair, as if to say, "These was you're doing." Whose would have thought he would turn out to be such a good hairdresser?

______________________________ ______________________________

______________________________ ______________________________

______________________________ ______________________________

____

Let's have fun!

Working out the missing **pronouns** in these sentences will help you complete the crossword puzzle.

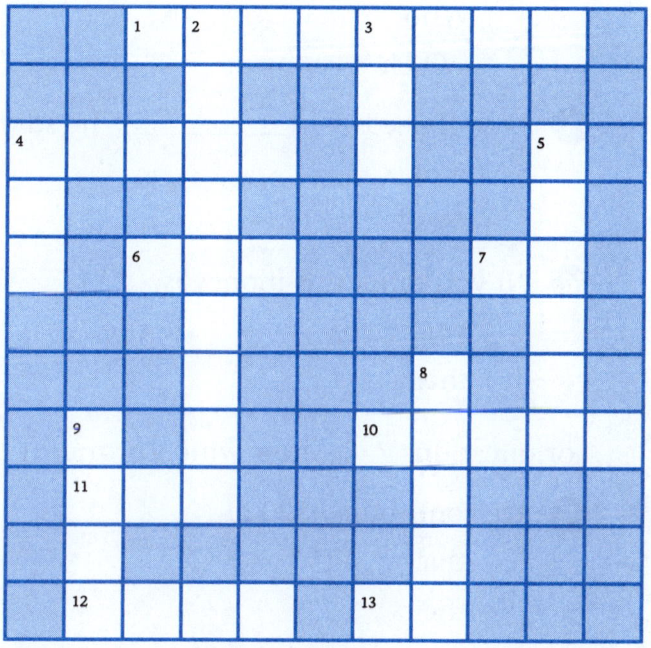

Across

1. If you want it done that way, you'll have to do it __________.
4. This is my desk and that is __________.
6. She thought __________ idea was better than his.
7. Paul said that _____ would help them.
10. "__________ hat is this?" asked the teacher.
11. "That's __________ hat," said the girl, pointing to Paul.
12. "I want _______ one over there," said the lady, pointing to the watermelon.
13. Jack and I said _____ would pay for it.

Down

2. When we turned right, we found __________ in a large hall.
3. "I think __________ knows the way," said Jack, pointing to Marcie.
4. "When are __________ going to do your homework?" asked Mum.
5. These aren't ours, so they must be __________.
8. "I'll take __________," Dad said as he picked up the shoes.
9. "__________ have you got to say for yourself?" asked the principal.

Let's have a test!

1. Which pronoun completes the sentence correctly?
The man gave ______________ each $2.
- ◯ him
- ◯ her
- ◯ us
- ◯ me

2. Which pronoun does **not** complete this sentence correctly?
I told her to give the extra money to ______________.
- ◯ them
- ◯ me
- ◯ him
- ◯ their

For questions 3–6, show which pronoun completes each sentence correctly.

3. We convinced ______________ that we could earn the money if we had to.
- ◯ ourselves
- ◯ yourselves
- ◯ themselves
- ◯ myself

4. "______________ are you going to do with all that money?" he asked.
- ◯ Who
- ◯ What
- ◯ Which
- ◯ Whose

5. "You'll need ______________," he said, handing me some money.
- ◯ that
- ◯ this
- ◯ these
- ◯ those

6. "If you think this money is ______________, you will have to prove it."
- ◯ your
- ◯ our
- ◯ their
- ◯ yours

For questions 7–8, show which pronoun does **not** complete each sentence correctly.

7. We contributed $20 to ______________ charity.
- ◯ their
- ◯ his
- ◯ theirs
- ◯ her

8. After we'd finished counting our money, we counted ______________.
- ◯ your
- ◯ theirs
- ◯ hers
- ◯ his

Let's write now!

Write a **narrative** about a boy or girl who finds an unusual way of earning some extra pocket money. In addition to **personal** and **possessive pronouns**, try to use at least one **reflexive pronoun**, one **interrogative pronoun** and one **demonstrative pronoun** in your narrative.

Unit 3 Memories

Focus

Adjectives

My favourite photograph

This photograph brings back happy memories. It's of a little girl in a **blue** bikini and a floppy hat shovelling sand into a plastic bucket. The little girl is me when I was five years old, and I'm sitting on a beach somewhere in northern Queensland. There are two seagulls on my right, and several palm trees behind me. It must have been a windy day, because the palm trees seem to be blowing about. I remember the seagulls. After Dad took the photo, they made off with my vegemite sandwiches and I burst into tears. Mum and Dad comforted me by buying me a chocolate ice-cream.

Of the **many** photos Mum and Dad took on that **December** holiday, this one is my favourite because I remember so clearly what happened on that day. I think it's a great photo!

by Nina

This is a **description**. A description helps us form mind pictures of people, places and things. Nina uses **adjectives** to give us more information about the people, places and things in the photograph she is describing.

Adjectives give more information about nouns or pronouns; for example, **blue** bikini, **many** photos, **December** holiday.

Adjectives make our writing more interesting, but we have to be careful how we use them.

Let's find them!

Find these nouns in the text.
Write the **adjective** that describes each noun.

1. memories ______________________
2. bucket ______________________
3. Queensland ______________________

Tip!

Don't use more than three **adjectives** to describe a noun or pronoun.

4. seagulls ______________________
5. palm trees ______________________
6. sandwiches ______________________
7. photo ______________________

Let's go to the next step!

Underline the **adjectives** in these sentences.
For example: I remember when I was awarded first prize in the dance competition.

1. Not all memories are good ones.
2. I love looking at the old photographs in Mum's big, wooden chest.
3. I have many memories of the time we spent with a Chinese family.
4. I remember when Grandpa gave me six little toy cars for my birthday.
5. My mother reminded me that I was also scared on my first day at school.
6. The large photograph in the silver frame is of my dad and me on our last fishing trip.
7. When I saw the colourful postcard, it brought back pleasant memories of our African safari.

Let's aim high now!

Choose the **adjective** that is opposite in meaning to the underlined one in each sentence and write it in the space.
For example: I have a gorgeous picture of myself at the funfair. horrible

cheap	boring	clear	straight	terrible	worthless	rough

1. I remember how curly my hair used to be. ______________________
2. He placed the photograph on the smooth surface. ______________________
3. Sometimes we forget how expensive holidays can be. ______________________
4. We had a wonderful time when we went to my uncle's farm. ______________________
5. I read an interesting story about a man who lost his memory. ______________________
6. My friend bought some valuable souvenirs when she was overseas. ______________________
7. She reminded her mother that they arrived in Melbourne on a rainy day. ______________________

The differences between Year 4 and Year 5

In my opinion, Year 5 is more interesting than Year 4, even though the work is **harder**. Last year I thought that Mrs Forbes was the **kindest** teacher I'd ever had, but Miss Laurie is just as kind. Our classroom this year is much brighter. It's also **more spacious**, even though the desks are bigger. One of the **most amazing** things about being in Year 5 is that we get to play on the basketball court at recess and lunch break.

I believe that each year is better than the last, and that next year will be the best of all. I remember how cool I thought the Year 5s were last year. Now that I'm in Year 5, I think the Year 6s are cool! But even though I'm not one of the oldest or biggest students in the school, I still feel more important than I did in Year 4.

by Damien

This is an **exposition**. An exposition expresses and gives reasons for an opinion, usually in order to convince others. Damien uses **adjectives** to compare Years 4 and 5 and to tell why he thinks Year 5 is better than Year 4.

Adjectives can compare people, places and things with each other; for example, Damien states that the work in Year 5 is **harder** than the work in Year 4.

Adjectives that compare are called **adjectives of degree**.

Rule!

- If two people, places or things are being compared, the adjective usually ends in *er*; for example, **hard<u>er</u>**. These are called **comparative adjectives**.
- If more than two people, animals, places or things are being compared, the adjective usually ends in *est*; for example, **kind<u>est</u>**. These are called **superlative adjectives**.
- When an adjective consists of more than two syllables, we use the word
  - » *more* in front of it when comparing two people, places or things; for example, **more spacious**.
  - » *most* in front of it when comparing more than two people, places or things; for example, **most amazing**.

Let's find them!

Find five **comparative adjectives** and three **superlative adjectives** in the text and write them in the spaces. Don't use the ones in bold.

1 ______________________________

2 ______________________________

Tip!

Some **adjectives of degree** don't follow the usual rules; for example,
good, better, best;
bad, worse, worst;
far, further, furthest;
little, less, least.

3. ______________________
4. ______________________
5. ______________________
6. ______________________
7. ______________________
8. ______________________

Let's go to the next step!

Complete this list of adjectives by filling in the **comparative** and **superlative** forms. The first two have been done for you.

Adjective	Comparative	Superlative
happy	happier	happiest
exciting	more exciting	most exciting
dangerous		
easy		
pretty		
brave		
beautiful		
lucky		
curious		
large		
tall		
peaceful		
busy		
young		

Let's aim high now!

Complete these sentences by choosing the correct form of the **adjectives** in brackets.
For example: I have (few) <u>fewer</u> memories than my grandparents.

1. That was the (bad) ______________ day of my life!
2. This photograph is (good) ______________ than that one.
3. Last year he was the (short) ______________ boy in the class.
4. My cat was once the (playful) ______________________ of all our pets.
5. I have (clear) ______________ memories of last year than the year before.
6. When I was three, I thought the moon was (big) ______________ than the sun.
7. The (incredible) ______________________ book I've ever read was about a man with a photographic memory.

Let's put it together now!

This student has written seven **adjectives** incorrectly in her description. Underline the mistakes and write the words correctly in the spaces below.

I have the more brilliant memories of the time we spent in the Australia outback last year. We travelled through a widest variety of landscapes, from dustier plains to rockiest mountain ranges, and each one seemed beautifuller than the last. It was definitely the good holiday I've ever had!

Let's have fun!

Fit these **adjectives** that Jenny used to describe her fifth birthday party into the spaces below.

new best older happiest delicious bright helpful delightful

Let's have a test!

For questions 1–2, choose the word that is an adjective in each sentence.

1 I remember several scenes from the film.

- ◯ remember
- ◯ several
- ◯ scenes
- ◯ film

2 She made a list because she is forgetful.

- ◯ made
- ◯ list
- ◯ because
- ◯ forgetful

3 Which sentence has been written correctly?

- ◯ This red little Chinese lantern reminds me of my holiday.
- ◯ This little Chinese red lantern reminds me of my holiday.
- ◯ This Chinese little red lantern reminds me of my holiday.
- ◯ This little red Chinese lantern reminds me of my holiday.

For questions 4–8, choose the word that completes the sentence correctly.

4 She was ____________ that he would remember her.

- ◯ hopeless
- ◯ hope
- ◯ hopeful
- ◯ hoped

5 His memory is better ____________ I thought.

- ◯ as
- ◯ than
- ◯ then
- ◯ like

6 She has ____________ memory in our family.

- ◯ worse
- ◯ worst
- ◯ the worst
- ◯ the worse

7 The town is ____________ away than I remember.

- ◯ far
- ◯ further
- ◯ furtherer
- ◯ more far

8 That was ____________ thing I've ever done!

- ◯ difficultest
- ◯ the difficultest
- ◯ most difficult
- ◯ the most difficult

Let's write now!

Answer one of the following:

1 Find a photograph of yourself as a young child and write a **description** of what you see. How old were you? What were you wearing? Who or what else is in the photograph?

2 Write a **comparison** between your life this year and last year. In what ways is your life similar and different?

Use **adjectives** to make your writing more interesting and to compare people, places and things.

Unit 4 Video and computer games

Focus
Verbs and verb groups

Are video and computer games bad for children?

Some people **think** that video and computer games **are** bad for children, while others believe they **have** a positive influence. I am going to look at both sides of the argument.

On the positive side, many video and computer games **teach** children life skills, such as how to care for pets. Others are educational and help children with their schoolwork. Some games improve thinking skills because they encourage children to sum up a situation and make quick decisions. They also develop hand-eye coordination.

On the other hand, many video and computer games have violence in them, which is not a good thing. Many people also say that in the past, children were healthier and used their imaginations more because they **played** outside and **read** more books rather than playing on a computer.

I believe that most video and computer games are good for children, as long as they don't spend too much time playing them. I love my games, and I **will continue** to play them.

by Cindy

This is a **discussion**. A discussion looks at both sides of an argument. Cindy uses **verbs** to tell what is happening and when it is happening while discussing the advantages and disadvantages of children playing computer games.

Verbs are the most important words in sentences. Without them, sentences don't make sense.

Verbs tell us what is happening. They can be
- doing words; for example, **think**.
- being words; for example, **are**.
- having words; for example, **have**.

Verbs also tell us when something happens.
- The **present tense** tells us that something is happening now; for example, Computer games **teach** children life skills.
- The **past tense** tells us that something has already happened; for example, In the past, children **played** outside.
- The **future tense** tells us that something has yet to happen; for example, I **will continue** to play them.

Rule!
- Most **past tense** verbs are formed by adding *d* or *ed* to the present form; for example, **played**.
- Some verbs change their spelling or pronunciation in the past tense; for example, **read**.
- The verbs **be**, **being**, **am**, **is** and **are** change to **been**, **was** and **were** in the past tense.
- The verbs **have** and **has** change to **had** in the past tense.
- **Future tense** verbs are formed by writing **will** or **am/are/is going to** before the present tense verb; for example, **I will continue to play them.**

Let's find them!

Underline the **verbs** in these sentences based on information in the text and state whether they are **present**, **past** or **future tense** verbs. The first one has been done for you.

1. Some computer games <u>improve</u> thinking skills. present tense
2. They also develop hand/eye coordination. ______________
3. Many computer games have violence in them. ______________
4. I will look at both sides of the argument. ______________
5. Children were healthier. ______________
6. Children used their imaginations more. ______________
7. I love my games. ______________

Let's go to the next step!

Complete this table by filling in the missing **verbs**. The first row has been done for you.

Present tense	Past tense	Future tense
compete	competed	will compete
buy		
		will make
watch		
	controlled	
		will move
win		
		will complete
		will allow
eat		

Let's aim high now!

Complete these sentences by choosing the correct **verb** from the brackets. Write the answers in the spaces.

1. Computer games (are/were/will be) ______________ very popular these days.
2. Right now, this (is/was/will be) ______________ my favourite computer game.
3. I (play/played/will play) ______________ computer games later.
4. The last time I counted, I (have/had/will have) ______________ twenty computer games.
5. My sister always (beats/beat/will beat) ______________ me when we play chess on the computer.
6. Yesterday my friend (show/showed/will show) ______________ me his new computer game.
7. Tomorrow my mum (take/took/will take) ______________ me to the shop to buy a new computer game.

How to play *Pac-Man*

One of my favourite computer games is *Pac-Man*. It **was released** in Japan in 1980 as an arcade game and is still popular today.

To earn points, the player must move Pac-Man through a maze of dots. If Pac-Man can eat all the dots, the player moves to the next level. Four ghosts **try to catch** Pac-Man. When one of them catches him, the player loses a life. When the player has lost three lives, the game is over.

The player must also earn points. One way of doing this is by eating the ghosts. When a ghost has been eaten, its eyes return to the centre of the screen and it regains its power. If a player manages to get 10000 points, they get a bonus life.

The first person to reach the maximum possible score of 3333360 points was from Florida in the United States. It took him almost six hours!

by Tristan

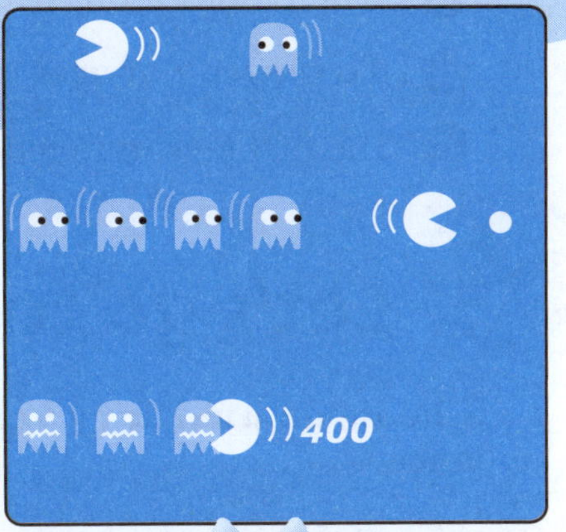

This is an **explanation**. An explanation tells why something happens or how it works. Tristan uses **verb groups** to explain what must be done to play the computer game, *Pac-Man*.

A **verb group** is a group of words that is built around a verb. Most verb groups are formed when one or more auxiliary or helping verbs is placed before the main verb; for example, **<u>was</u> released**.

These are the **auxiliary verbs**:

am → are, be → been, can → could, did → do → does, had → has, have → is, may → might → must, shall → should, was → were, will → would

Verb groups are also formed by
- placing **to** before a verb; for example, **to earn**. (This is known as an **infinitive**.)
- placing an infinitive and other verbs next to each other; for example, **try to catch**.

Let's find them!

Find the **verb groups** in these sentences based on information in the text and underline them. The first one has been done for you.

Tip!
A common mistake is to write **could of** and **would of** instead of **could have** and **would have**. Be careful not to make this mistake!

1. The player <u>must move</u> Pac-Man through a maze of dots.
2. If Pac-Man can eat all the dots, the player moves to the next level.
3. When the player has lost three lives, the game is over.
4. The player must earn points.

5. When a ghost has been eaten, its eyes return to the centre of the screen.
6. If a player manages to get 10 000 points, they get a bonus life.
7. The first person to reach that score was from Florida.

Let's go to the next step!

Choose an **auxiliary verb** from the box to complete these sentences. Use each word once.

could   must   has   have   am   are   should

1. She ______________ beat her old score this time.
2. I think I ______________ played this computer game before.
3. You ______________ try harder if you want to beat his score.
4. I ______________ get a higher score if I concentrate harder.
5. We ______________ going to get a new game console for Christmas.
6. This is a very difficult game, but I ______________ getting better at it.
7. He ______________ bought two more computer games to add to his collection.

Let's aim high now!

Complete each sentence with a **verb group** from the box. Use each verb group once.

have done   could play   has destroyed
will get   might buy   are aiming
does play

Tip!
Read through the sentences before you start filling in your answers!

1. My little brother ______________________ my game console.
2. Grandpa says he ______________________ me that computer game.
3. I ______________________ a higher score if no one interrupts me.
4. He ______________________ computer games, doesn't he?
5. My friend and I ______________________ for 10 000 points on this game.
6. I asked her if I ______________________ computer games for half an hour a day.
7. Mum lets me play computer games when I ______________________ all my chores.

Let's put it together now!

This student has written some **verbs** and **verb groups** incorrectly in this part of his explanation. Use a red pen to make the corrections for him.

The first Mario Kart computer game is launched in 1992. Since then, Nintendo has released many more versions of the game.

Mario Kart have four modes—Grand Prix, Vs, Time Trial and Battle. In the Grand Prix and Vs modes, the player must raced against other players, while in the Time Trial mode, the player have to finish the course as quickly as possible. In Battle mode, the players get a certain number of balloons. They lost a balloon every time someone hits them. The player that are left with the most balloons is the winner.

Mario Kart is my favourite computer game. I hope there may be many more versions of the game in the future.

Let's have fun!

Write the **past tense** of these **verbs** in the spaces, then circle the letter indicated by the number beside each verb; for example:

write wrote 2nd

The circled letters spell the name of a popular computer game.

Present tense	**Past tense**	**Circle this letter**
1 sit	____________	1st
2 can	____________	3rd
3 clap	____________	5th
4 are	____________	4th
5 hear	____________	4th
6 come	____________	3rd
7 begin	____________	4th
8 strike	____________	3rd
9 say	____________	3rd
10 break	____________	3rd

Answer: The name of the computer game is ____________ ____________

Let's have a test!

In questions 1–8, choose the word or words that complete each sentence correctly.

1. My little sister ______________ to use the computer.
   - ◯ try
   - ◯ try's
   - ◯ tries
   - ◯ trying

2. My new computer game ______________ on the shelf.
   - ◯ is
   - ◯ am
   - ◯ are
   - ◯ were

3. Last year he ______________ ten computer games.
   - ◯ has
   - ◯ have
   - ◯ had
   - ◯ will have

4. I ______________ a new computer game tomorrow.
   - ◯ got
   - ◯ getting
   - ◯ will get
   - ◯ going to get

5. I ______________ asked him how to play the game.
   - ◯ should
   - ◯ should of
   - ◯ should has
   - ◯ should have

6. I have tried ______________ that game before.
   - ◯ play
   - ◯ played
   - ◯ to play
   - ◯ can play

7. I ______________ all night if Mum hadn't stopped me.
   - ◯ would play
   - ◯ would played
   - ◯ would of played
   - ◯ would have played

8. He ______________ that game!
   - ◯ should won
   - ◯ should of won
   - ◯ should have won
   - ◯ should have win

Let's write now!

Answer one of the following.

1. **Discuss** the advantages and disadvantages of children being allowed to take their game consoles, such as a DS or PlayStation, to school.
2. Choose a video or computer game that you enjoy playing and **explain** how it works.

Use a variety of **verbs** and **verb groups** in your **discussion** or **explanation**.

Unit 5 Optical illusions

Focus
Verbal adjectives; verbal nouns

How optical illusions work

An optical illusion is when we see something that doesn't exist, or that looks different from what it actually is. An example of this is when you are travelling on a long, straight road on a hot, sunny day and you see what looks like water in the distance. This is called a mirage. It happens when hot air meets cold air. **Refracting light** makes it appear as if the road is reflecting the sky.

Some optical illusions are created deliberately. Many of these images have become famous. They are fun to look at and they can lead to **improved concentration**. In some optical illusions we see disappearing dots, moving circles, changing colours and images hiding in other images. For example, if we have stimulated our brains too much, such as by looking at bright colours, we see after-images that are not really there.

I have made this optical illusion for you. Do you see a rabbit, or a duck?

by Martin

This is an **explanation**. Remember: an explanation tells us why things happen or how they work. Martin uses **verbal adjectives** to give more information about nouns while explaining how optical illusions work.

Verbal adjectives are verbs that are used as adjectives. Like adjectives, they give more information about nouns.

Verbal adjectives end in
- *ing*; for example, **Refracting light**.
- *ed*; for example, **improved concentration**.

Let's find them!

Find these words in the text and write down whether they are being used as **verbs** or **adjectives**. Remember: adjectives describe something.

1. travelling ______________________
2. reflecting ______________________
3. disappearing ______________________
4. moving ______________________
5. changing ______________________
6. hiding ______________________

Let's go to the next step!

Complete these sentences by filling in a **verbal adjective** from the box.

roasted	howling	flying	sloping	haunted	sinking	exciting

1. The ________________ aeroplane is an optical illusion.
2. He pretended to be a ghost in a ________________ house.
3. The illusionist is planning an ________________ new show.
4. My sister thought that the ________________ wind was a monster.
5. Not all people can see the ________________ ship in the image.
6. The illusionist offered me a packet of ________________ peanuts.
7. He created an illusion in which the ________________ floor looked level.

Let's aim high now!

Add the suffix *ing* or *ed* to the **verbs** in brackets to turn them into **adjectives**; for example: He showed the (bore) bored class a magic trick.

Rule!

For verbs that end in *y*, change *y* to *i* before adding *ed*; for example, **fry → fried**.

For verbs that end in *e*, drop the *e* before adding *ing*; for example, **close → closing**.

For verbs that already have an *e* at the end, just add *d*; for example, **close → closed**.

For verbs that have a short vowel before the final consonant, double the consonant before adding *ing* or *ed*; for example, **rip → ripping → ripped**.

1. The (leak) ________________ tap is not an optical illusion!
2. He uses a (boil) ________________ egg in one of his tricks.
3. She seemed to be wearing a (knit) ________________ jacket.
4. His (talk) ________________ puppet is the star of the show!
5. The illusionist put on an (entertain) ________________ show.
6. The magician put the (chop) ________________ onion back together.
7. He took a (crumple) ________________ scarf out of the magician's hat.

How to create an optical illusion

Drawing is fun. Creating optical illusions is even more fun, and drawing them is easier than you think. All you need to create this optical illusion is a black pen, an A4 sheet of paper and a ruler.

Start by folding the paper in half.

Next, draw a small circle in the centre of the paper.

Using your ruler, draw straight lines through the circle so they form a cross. Fill in the spaces with more lines that radiate outwards from the centre (see diagram).

After measuring and marking points exactly one centimetre on either side of the small circle, draw parallel lines through the larger circle.

You know that the two lines you have just drawn are straight, but looking at them, you'd think they were curved.

Optical illusions prove that seeing is not always believing!

by Freya

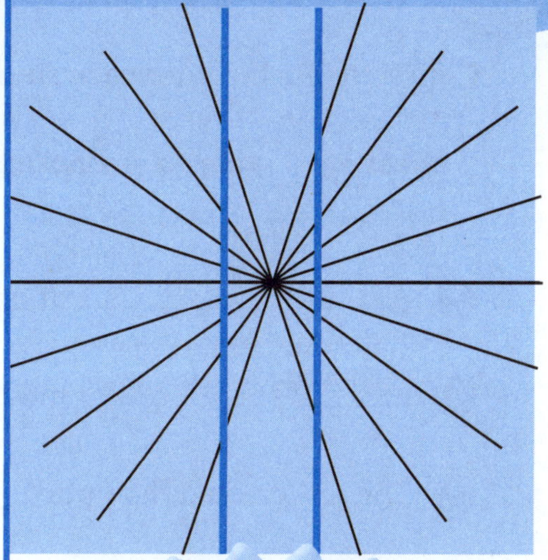

This is a **procedure**. A procedure gives instructions on how to do or make something. Freya uses **verbal nouns** to name actions while giving instructions on how to create an optical illusion.

Verbal nouns are *ing* forms of the verb that do the work of **nouns**—that is, they name actions; for example, **Drawing is fun.**

Let's find them!

Find eight **verbal nouns** in the text and write them in the spaces. Don't use the one in bold.

1. ____________________
2. ____________________
3. ____________________
4. ____________________
5. ____________________
6. ____________________
7. ____________________
8. ____________________

Let's go to the next step!

Complete each sentence with a **verbal noun** from the box.

cheering	ringing	looking	performing	murmuring	following	queuing

1. ________________ at optical illusions is his favourite pastime.
2. ________________ magic tricks successfully requires great skill.
3. The girl created the optical illusion by ________________ the instructions.
4. Each of the illusionist's tricks was followed by enthusiastic ________________.
5. The ________________ of the bell told us that the magic show was about to start.
6. I looked at the program while ________________ for tickets to see the magic show.
7. A soft ________________ could be heard when the illusionist made the man disappear.

Let's aim high now!

Match these sentence beginnings with their endings. Underline the **verbal nouns**.

Sentence beginning	Sentence ending
1 The magician created the illusion by using	by telling them a joke.
2 Sitting in the front row,	a card up my sleeve.
3 The trick failed because of	they finally mastered the trick.
4 The illusionist distracted the audience	revealing his secret.
5 The magician showed us the trick without	a set of mirrors.
6 I have learnt how to create an illusion by hiding	the illusionist's fumbling.
7 After practising for hours every day,	I could see exactly what the illusionist was doing.

Let's put it together now!

This student should have added ***ing*** or ***ed*** to the underlined words in this procedure. Fill in the corrections for him.

Creating a rainbow wheel

Make ____________________ this interest ____________________ illusion is simple.

You will need a paper plate; white craft paper; colour ____________________ pencils, crayons or markers; a ruler; some tape; and scissors.

Trace the paper plate onto the cardboard and then cut out the circle.

Next, divide the circle into eight equal sections and colour each section a different colour.

Use ____________________ your scissors, make a small hole in the centre of your complete ____________________ circle. Insert a pencil in the hole and keep it secure by tape ____________________ it in place.

Twirl the pencil between your palms to create a spin ____________________ motion. What do you see?

Let's have fun!

These **verbal adjectives** and **verbal nouns** are hiding in the wordsearch puzzle:

finished cooked watching vanishing painted hopping sitting flying

Can you find them? The words go forwards, backwards, up and down.

x	s	t	v	a	n	i	s	h	i	n	g	v	a	o
c	i	x	v	w	q	h	y	h	o	p	p	i	n	g
h	t	b	a	s	s	q	j	f	n	d	z	n	f	d
d	t	j	g	n	i	y	l	f	h	e	r	d	j	k
l	i	r	w	c	n	w	f	h	j	h	z	e	m	o
e	n	q	v	a	q	r	h	j	d	s	h	t	i	k
h	g	t	i	h	g	f	h	s	h	i	g	n	g	d
a	f	j	n	n	z	x	n	v	s	n	w	i	r	t
g	n	i	h	c	t	a	w	h	h	i	k	a	c	x
a	f	e	y	u	w	y	u	h	k	f	b	p	b	p
z	y	r	d	e	k	o	o	c	i	p	u	h	d	a

Let's have a test!

In questions 1–8, which word completes each sentence correctly?

1. He is an ______________ illusionist.
   - ◯ amaze
   - ◯ amazing
   - ◯ good
   - ◯ wonderful

2. The ______________ lady agreed to help the illusionist.
   - ◯ scare
   - ◯ scaring
   - ◯ scared
   - ◯ scares

3. I have been to many ______________ magic shows.
   - ◯ boring
   - ◯ bored
   - ◯ bores
   - ◯ bore

4. The magician found the ______________ coin behind my ear.
   - ◯ miss
   - ◯ missing
   - ◯ misses
   - ◯ mist

5. ______________ for the show to start, the audience chatted among themselves.
   - ◯ Wait
   - ◯ Waited
   - ◯ Waiting
   - ◯ Waits

6. ______________ magic shows is fascinating.
   - ◯ Watch
   - ◯ Watches
   - ◯ Watched
   - ◯ Watching

7. The magician's hobby is ______________.
   - ◯ swimming
   - ◯ swum
   - ◯ swam
   - ◯ swim

8. ______________ his wand, the magician made the rabbit reappear.
   - ◯ Waved
   - ◯ Waveing
   - ◯ Waving
   - ◯ Waves

Let's write now!

Look in books or on the Internet for an optical illusion that is easy to draw. Write a **procedure** giving instructions on how to draw it. Use **verbal adjectives** and **verbal nouns** in your procedure.

Unit 6 Fables

Focus

Adverbs

The boy who cried wolf

There was once a boy whose job it was to look after the village flock. He **dutifully** took the sheep out into the fields **early** in the morning, and brought them back when the sun went **down**. He **occasionally** amused himself by carving a piece of wood or watching a little animal go about its business, but mostly he got bored during the day. And so it was that one afternoon he decided to play a trick on the villagers. He ran to the village and called out loudly, "Wolf! Wolf!" before hurrying back to the flock.

The villagers quickly ran after the boy, only to find that he had tricked them. The boy was **very** pleased with himself and decided to repeat the trick the following day.

Again, when the villagers ran to save their animals they saw that the boy had tricked them. They scolded him angrily before returning to their chores.

The following day a wolf really did attack the flock. When the boy called for help, the villagers ignored him. He had tricked them once too often!

by Lavinia

This is a fable. A fable is a **narrative** that contains a moral, or lesson. Lavinia uses **adverbs** to add information about verbs in this fable about the boy who cried wolf.

Adverbs add information about verbs. They tell us

- how something happens or is done; for example, **dutifully** (manner). They include words like *softly*, *slowly*, *freshly*, *happily* and *sadly*.
- when something happens; for example, **early** (time). They include words like *immediately*, *lately*, *soon*, *yesterday* and *tomorrow*.
- where something happens; for example, **down** (place). They include words like *near*, *here*, *there*, *up* and *away*.
- how often something happens; for example, **occasionally** (frequency). They include words like *always*, *never*, *sometimes*, *seldom* and *rarely*.
- to what extent something happens; for example, **very** (degree). They include words like *extremely*, *hardly*, *nearly*, *quite* and *almost*.

Let's find them!

Find these **adverbs** in the text and write down what type of adverb it is. The first one has been done for you.

1. mostly frequency
2. back ______
3. loudly ______
4. again ______
5. angrily ______
6. really ______
7. often ______

Let's go to the next step!

Complete each sentence with an **adverb** from the box.

seldom hardly sadly away yesterday brightly lately properly

1. The boy cried "Wolf" for the last time ______.
2. The boy looked ______ at the slaughtered sheep.
3. The sun was shining ______ when the wolf attacked the sheep.
4. Some of the sheep tried to run ______ when they saw the wolf.
5. The villagers ______ listened to the boy the third time he called "Wolf".
6. ______ the boy has not been looking after the sheep ______.
7. Fables are meant to teach us lessons, but people ______ learn from them.

Let's aim high now!

Underline the **adverb** in each of these sentences and write down what type of adverb it is.

For example: The boy sobbed bitterly when the wolf killed his sheep. manner

1. The wolf eyed the sheep greedily. ______
2. The girl left the book of fables here. ______
3. The boy knew that there was a wolf nearby. ______
4. The shepherd ran enthusiastically to his flock. ______
5. The boy immediately ran to warn the villagers. ______
6. I have almost finished reading the book of fables. ______
7. The fable teaches us that people never listen to a liar. ______

The fox and the goat

One day a fox fell into a well. He managed to find a ledge to sit on, but although he was **fairly comfortable**, he was also anxious. How was he going to get out of the well?

Sometime later he heard a bleating sound above him. He looked up and saw an extremely large goat looking down at him. The fox immediately thought of a plan to trick the goat into helping him escape.

"Mmmhmmm!" he exclaimed. "This is the sweetest water I have ever tasted. Come and try it."

The goat, who was exceedingly thirsty, jumped into the well. Pretty soon he, too, realised that he was trapped. The fox assured him that he had a plan to get them out of the well. He convinced the goat that because he could **jump higher** and run faster, he should be the one to get out first and go for help. The goat, who was rather stupid, believed the fox. He put his forepaws up against the wall (as the fox had told him to do) and turned his body into a ladder for the fox to scramble up.

When the fox was safely out of the well, he bounded off, quite oblivious to the pitiful bleating of the goat. Fortunately a farmer came by shortly afterwards and rescued the goat, who had learnt a valuable lesson—**think more carefully** before jumping into something!

by Dylan

This is another fable. Dylan uses **adverbs** to describe adjectives and other adverbs, and to compare the way in which actions are performed in this story about a fox and a goat.

Adverbs can also be used to describe
- an adjective; for example, **fairly comfortable**.
- another adverb; for example, **Sometime later**.

Like adjectives, adverbs have comparative and superlative forms to show degree; for example, **jump higher**/**think more carefully**.

Let's find them!

Find these **adverbs** in the text and write down on the next page whether they are describing an adjective, describing another adverb, or comparing two or more ways of doing something. The first one has been done for you.

Tip!

While some **comparative** and **superlative adverbs** take ***er*** and ***est***, more have the words **more**, **most**, **less** or **least** in front of them; for example, **more carefully**.

1. extremely describing an adjective
2. exceedingly ______
3. pretty ______
4. faster ______
5. rather ______
6. quite ______
7. shortly ______

Let's go to the next step!

Choose the word in brackets that completes each sentence correctly. Make sure the word is an **adverb**! Cross out the words that are incorrect.
For example: The wolf moved (more quickly/~~most quickly~~) than the sheep.

1. The villagers very (near/nearly) lost their entire flock.
2. The wolf had (most/almost) never had so much to eat.
3. The boy tried (really/real) hard to get the villagers' attention.
4. The boy has (more certainly/most certainly) learned his lesson.
5. The fox was (to/too/two) far away to hear the goat's angry bleating.
6. The fox handled the situation (cleverly/more cleverly) than the goat.
7. The fox said that he could get out (easier/more easily) than the goat.

Let's aim high now!

Complete these sentences with an **adverb** from the box. Use each word once.

often	confidently	fairly	closer	carefully	stupidly	extremely

1. The wolf crept ever ______ to the sheep.
2. The boy quite ______ left the sheep unattended.
3. The boy watched the sheep more ______ after that.
4. The goat acted rather ______ by jumping into the well.
5. That fable has an ______ important lesson to teach us.
6. The farmer was ______ certain that the bleating was coming from the well.
7. The wolf approached the flock less ______ when the shepherd was nearby.

Let's put it together now!

This student has written seven **adverbs** incorrectly in her retelling of the fable, *The Hare and the Tortoise*. Underline the mistakes and write the corrections in the spaces below.

One day a tortoise challenged a hare to a race. The hare thought the tortoise was being utter ridiculous and laughed loud. Nevertheless, he accepted the tortoise's challenge and the two lined up. The hare, who could run much fastest than the tortoise, raced ahead. He got so further ahead of the tortoise that he decided to have a nap, believing that he would still have lots of time to get to the finish line before his rival. But the hare slept most deeply than he expected, and while he was sleeping, the tortoise plodded on steady. When the hare woke up, the tortoise was nearing the finish line. The hare tried to catch up, but the tortoise beat him easy.

____________________ ____________________

____________________ ____________________

____________________ ____________________

____

Let's have fun!

Complete the **adverbs** in these sentences by picking letters from the jar. There are twenty-one letters in the jar, one for each space. Each time you use a letter, cross it off. There shouldn't be any letters left by the time you have filled in all the spaces.

The tortoise moved more s ___ o ___ ___ y than the hare.

S ___ m e ___ ___ m ___ s the boy got bored while watching the sheep.

Fables are m ___ s t ___ y about animals.

Fables a ___ w ___ y ___ teach us a lesson.

The lion roared a ___ g ___ i l ___ when it stepped on a thorn.

The hare was ___ e ___ y disappointed when he lost the race.

I am q ___ i ___ e sure that the hare would have won if he hadn't gone to sleep.

The tortoise crossed the line first, and the hare followed s ___ o ___ afterwards.

Let's have a test!

1. Which sentence tells how often the action is done?
   - ◯ The girl willingly read the book of fables.
   - ◯ The girl frequently reads the book of fables.
   - ◯ The girl is reading the book of fables now.
   - ◯ The girl is reading the book of fables outside.

2. Which sentence tells when the action is done?
   - ◯ I have read this fable before.
   - ◯ I have never read this fable.
   - ◯ I've seen this fable somewhere.
   - ◯ I read the fable quietly.

3. Which sentence tells where the action is done?
   - ◯ The wolf is always watching.
   - ◯ The wolf is watching now.
   - ◯ The wolf is watching patiently.
   - ◯ The wolf is watching nearby.

4. Which sentence tells how the action is done?
   - ◯ The sheep soon bleated.
   - ◯ The sheep bleated sometimes.
   - ◯ The sheep bleated helplessly.
   - ◯ The sheep bleated immediately.

For questions 5–8, show which option completes the sentences correctly.

5. The shepherd ____________ ever left his sheep.
   - ◯ harder
   - ◯ hardly
   - ◯ hardest
   - ◯ hard

6. The boy did an ____________ silly thing.
   - ◯ very
   - ◯ quite
   - ◯ really
   - ◯ extremely

7. The fox landed ____________ than he expected.
   - ◯ heavier
   - ◯ heavily
   - ◯ more heavily
   - ◯ most heavily

8. The goat will ____________ never listen to the fox again.
   - ◯ more likely
   - ◯ most likely
   - ◯ likelier
   - ◯ likeliest

Let's write now!

Find a **fable** in a book or on the Internet and rewrite it in your own words. Use as many different types of **adverbs** as possible in your story.

Unit 7 Inventions that have changed the way we live

Focus

Prepositions; adverbial phrases

The invention of the wheel

A wheel attached **to** an axle was recently found in Slovenia. Tests showed that it dated from 3100 BCE! We might not know who invented the wheel, but we do know that it's been around for a very long time.

The discovery of the wheel and axle made it easier to transport people and goods. Without the wheel, we wouldn't have motor cars, aeroplanes and the thousands of other machines that make our lives easier. Even during ancient times, people were able to create quite complicated machines using the wheel. The most important were those used to lift weights.

The wheel was discovered before the light bulb, telephone and all the other inventions that have changed the way we live. We have to ask ourselves—would these discoveries have been possible if humans had never developed the wheel?

by Vicky

This is a **report**. A report gives factual information about people or things. In this report about the invention of the wheel, Vicky uses **prepositions** to show the relationship between nouns, pronouns and other words in the sentence.

Prepositions show relationships between nouns or pronouns and other words in the sentence; for example, **to** shows the relationship between the wheel and the axle.

Here is a list of prepositions:

about, above, across, after, against, along, as, at, before, behind, below, beneath, beside, between, by, down, during, for, from, in, inside, into, near, of, off, on, onto, over, past, round, since, through, to, towards, under, until, up, with, without.

Let's find them!

Find six different **prepositions** in the text and write them in the spaces below. Don't use the one in bold.

1. ______________________
2. ______________________
3. ______________________
4. ______________________
5. ______________________
6. ______________________

Let's go to the next step!

Complete each sentence with a **preposition** from the box. Use each word once.

by	since	on	before	in	beside	to	above	about

1. He hasn't developed a new invention ____________ last April.
2. The battery-operated car was built ____________ a famous inventor.
3. I wish someone would invent a toy that could talk ____________ me!
4. I placed my invention ____________ hers ____________ the table.
5. I often see the famous inventor walking ____________ ____________ his garden.
6. Thomas Edison tried and failed many times ____________ perfecting the light bulb.
7. When I looked up, I saw his new invention hovering ____________ my head.

Let's aim high now!

Cross out the **preposition** in brackets that doesn't complete the sentence correctly.
For example: The inventor locked himself (in, ~~into~~, inside) his laboratory.

1. I've heard (to, of, about) the new invention.
2. This new invention is (for, from, of) my sister.
3. My robot groans very time I switch it (on, of, off).
4. I put the new mixture I invented (under, on, in) the table.
5. I was horrified when I saw the robot gobbling (in, up, down) the inventor's hat!
6. When I looked (by, through, out) the window, I saw the inventor testing his new bicycle.
7. My teacher walked (by, between, past) just as I was putting the finishing touches (to, on, of) my invention.

The invention of the internet

The invention that has had the greatest impact **on people's lives** in recent years is the internet. It is popular with people of all ages as it allows them to access information across the world at all times. I am 10 years old and I spend almost as much time browsing the net as I do watching television.

In the 1960s, the United States Army developed computers that could 'talk' to each other. At first they were used only for research, but soon more computer networks were developed in other places and by the 1990s, we had the internet.

Many people believe that because of the speed at which the internet works, it will help us discover lots of new inventions in the future.

by Matt

This is another **report**. Matt uses **adverbial phrases** to give more information about verbs in this report on the invention of the internet.

Phrases
- are groups of words that form part of a sentence.
- do not contain a verb.
- often start with a **preposition**; for example, **on people's lives**.

Adverbial phrases are phrases that do the work of adverbs—that is, they give more information about verbs. They tell us
- how something is done; for example, He answered with a smile.
- where something is done; for example, She lives in the United States.
- when something is done; for example, They developed it during the last century.
- why something is done; for example, He did it for no good reason.
- how often something is done; for example, I can see him at certain times.
- to what extent something is done; for example, She works with extreme care.

Let's find them!

Find these **adverbial phrases** in the text and write down whether they tell where, when, why or how often something is done.

1. in recent years ______________________
2. across the world ______________________
3. at all times ______________________
4. In the 1960s ______________________
5. for research ______________________
6. in other places ______________________
7. in the future ______________________

Let's go to the next step!

Underline the **adverbial phrases** in these sentences.
For example: I found the information on the Internet.

1. I amazed everyone with my new invention.
2. He goes to his laboratory as often as possible.
3. In the future, someone might invent a flying car.
4. The inventor has a laboratory behind his house.
5. The instrument she invented works better than his.
6. We saw the latest gadgets at the International Inventors' Fair.
7. When my dad test-drove the new car, he wanted it more than ever.

Let's aim high now!

Complete these sentences with an **adverbial phrase** from the box and write down whether it tells us how, when, where, how often or to what extent the action is being done.

For example: We work on our experiments every other day. How often

with much greater speed	in the rubbish bin	now and again
at about six o'clock	onto the stage	without difficulty
for hours on end		

1. The first thing I ever invented ended up ____________________. __________
2. I could talk about my inventions ____________________. __________
3. Using the new invention, they were able to finish the task ____________________. __________
4. The inventor walked ____________________ to accept his award. __________
5. This new invention will allow us to move ____________________ than before. __________
6. Not all of his inventions are practical, but ____________________ he comes up with a good one. __________
7. The scientist left his laboratory ____________________ and arrived home an hour later. __________

Let's put it together now!

This student has written seven **prepositions** incorrectly in this section of his report. Underline them and write the corrections in the spaces below.

Bicycles have had a huge impact in people's lives since they were first invented on the 19th century. In some countries, they are still the main form off transport, while in others they are used mainly from recreation. The first two-wheel vehicle was invented about the German, Baron Karl Vondrais. The wheels, which weren't the same size, were attached towards a wooden frame. The bicycle didn't have pedals. The rider had to push the bicycle forward without his feet.

Let's have fun!

All of the words that complete this puzzle are **prepositions**. The sentences will help you work out which ones they are.

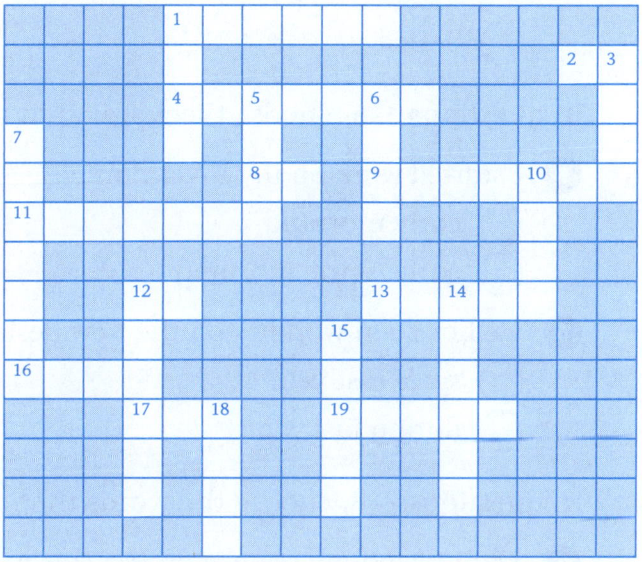

Across

1. The vacuum cleaner is ______ the cupboard.
2. I climbed ______ the ladder.
4. The bus was heading ______ us.
8. I gave my invention ____ my teacher.
9. Today we find it difficult to be ______ electricity.
11. I can see the stars when I look ______ a telescope.
12. My alarm clock rings ____ six o'clock.
13. Dad keeps his exercise machine ______ the bed.
16. The inventor's laboratory is ______ his house.
17. I took my invention ______ the table.
19. You'll have to wait ______ tomorrow to see her new invention.

Down

1. The inventor invited us ______ his workshop.
3. When we walked ____ the robot, it said "Good morning"!
5. I brush my teeth ____ an electric toothbrush.
6. He rides up and ____ the street on his new bicycle.
7. The inventor stood ____ his two robots.
10. I thought the book about famous inventors was ____ there.
12. He stuck a strip of plastic ____ the robot's back.
14. She works on her inventions ____ the holidays.
15. The robot is walking ____ the room.
18. This new type of washing machine comes ____ Europe.

Let's have a test!

1 Which sentence has been written correctly?

- I left my invention in school.
- I left my invention at school.
- I left my invention by school.
- I left my invention on school.

In questions 2–3, choose the word that completes the sentence correctly.

2 I gave the invention ______ my mother.

- from
- for
- at
- to

3 I made the robot ______ my little brother.

- for
- from
- to
- by

4 Which word does **not** complete this sentence correctly?

I found the inventor's notes ______ the drawer.

- inside
- in
- beside
- for

In questions 5–6, choose the words that complete the sentence correctly.

5 I started work on my invention ____________.

- early morning
- early in morning
- early in the morning
- early the morning

6 He has been working on the new design ____________.

- since last year
- until last year
- during last year
- about last year.

In questions 7–8, choose the words that do **not** complete the sentence correctly.

7 I completed my science project this morning ____________.

- before the sun came up
- after the sun came up
- when the sun came up
- past the sun came up

8 My dad tried out his new invention ____________.

- to the park
- in the park
- near the park
- at the park

Let's write now!

Look in books or on the Internet for information about an invention that has changed the world. Examples include the electric light bulb, the motor car and the steam engine. Write a **report** about the invention you have chosen. Use **prepositions** and **adverbial phrases** in your report.

Unit 8 Food from around the world

Focus
Adjectival phrases; commas

A visit to a Thai restaurant

Last week my family and I went to the new Thai restaurant **in Fern Hill**. The owner, in a traditional Thai sarong, met us at the door. He showed us to a table next to the window and asked a waiter to bring us a jug of water. The food on the menu looked delicious and I didn't know what to choose. Finally I ordered spring rolls and a stir fry with noodles. The vegetables inside the spring rolls were fresh and crispy and the stir fry was spicy and delicious. I also ordered apple juice in a tall glass. We all enjoyed the meal and will definitely be going back to that restaurant.

by Iris

This is a **recount**. Remember: a recount tells about things that have already happened. Iris uses **adjectival phrases** to give more information about nouns and pronouns in this recount of her visit to a Thai restaurant.

Adjectival phrases

- are groups of words in a sentence.
- do not contain a verb.
- can start with a preposition, verbal noun or infinitive.
- give more information about nouns or pronouns; for example, **in Fern Hill** gives more information about the new Thai restaurant.

Let's find them!

Find the **adjectival phrases** in the text that give more information about these nouns.

1. owner ______________________
2. table ______________________
3. jug ______________________
4. food ______________________

5 stir fry ______________________________

6 vegetables ______________________________

7 apple juice ______________________________

Let's go to the next step!

Underline the **adjectival phrases** in these sentences.
For example: People from foreign countries like our food.

1 I prefer eating fruits without seeds.

2 The chef uses coriander from his garden.

3 Thai food is a mixture of different flavours.

4 The chef in the tall hat makes amazing food.

5 The bottle behind the vinegar contains fish sauce.

6 The restaurant down the road makes delicious spring rolls.

7 The customers near the window have ordered Tom Yum Soup.

Let's aim high now!

Complete each sentence with an **adjectival phrase** from the box.
Use each phrase once.

serving the food	in the pot	covered in sauce
with deep pockets	at the Chinese restaurant	of chocolates
	on the tables	

1 I bought the box ______________________________ in Switzerland.

2 The tea ______________________________ comes from Japan.

3 The lady ______________________________ is the owner's wife.

4 The meat ______________________________ looks like chicken.

5 The cloths ______________________________ are brightly coloured.

6 The apron ______________________________ belongs to the chef.

7 The food ______________________________ is excellent.

Spaghetti and meatballs in tomato sauce

Both the adults and the children in your house will love these tasty meatballs with spaghetti and tomato sauce.

To make this dish, you will need the following ingredients: 500 g minced beef, a jar of spaghetti sauce, an egg, a small handful of breadcrumbs, a chopped garlic clove, a teaspoon of salt, a handful of grated cheese and 500 g spaghetti.

Method:

1. Cook the spaghetti, following the directions on the packet.
2. Place the sauce in a large saucepan and heat it over a medium heat.
3. In a large bowl, mix together the **beef, egg and breadcrumbs**.
4. **When thoroughly mixed, add the** garlic, salt and cheese and combine well. Shape into small balls.
5. Place the meatballs in the sauce and let it simmer for at least 40 minutes.
6. Serve the meatballs and sauce over the spaghetti.

This is a **recipe**, which is a type of procedure. A procedure tells how to make or do something. The writer uses **commas** to make the meaning of sentences clearer while telling how to make spaghetti and meatballs in tomato sauce.

Commas make the meaning of sentences clearer. They are used to

- separate nouns, adjectives or actions in a list; for example, **beef, egg and breadcrumbs**.
- separate phrases from the rest of the sentence; for example, **When thoroughly mixed, add the ...**

Let's find them!

Tip!

Remember: the last two items in a list are separated by **and/or** without a comma.

Fill in the missing **commas** in these sentences based on information in the text.

1. To make this dish you will need lots of ingredients.
2. The recipe uses minced beef spaghetti sauce and an egg.

3. It also uses breadcrumbs garlic salt cheese and spaghetti.
4. Prepare the spaghetti following the directions on the packet.
5. In a large bowl combine the remaining ingredients.
6. After that place the meatballs in the sauce.
7. When cooked serve the meatballs and sauce over the spaghetti.

Let's go to the next step!

Underline the lists in these sentences. Remember: **commas** can separate items in a list. For example: I like Thai, Italian and Greek food.

1. I had sushi, an apple and a fruit drink for lunch.
2. You can buy pizzas in supermarkets, bakeries and restaurants.
3. The vegetables on my plate were green, orange, red and yellow.
4. There were knives, forks, spoons, plates and glasses on the table.
5. The chef peeled the potatoes, chopped the vegetables and prepared the sauce.
6. I helped Mum by setting the table, packing away the dishes and making the tea.
7. The restaurant was decorated with little fountains, statues and paintings of people eating.

Let's aim high now!

Fill in the missing **commas** in these sentences.

1. To my horror they offered me stink bugs to eat!
2. Without a doubt the food from Korea is the tastiest.
3. They used vegetables herbs and spices in that dish.
4. Some people don't like ice-cream chocolate or cake!
5. I have eaten food from Italy Greece Vietnam and China.
6. I never add salt pepper vinegar or tomato sauce to my food.
7. Thai food with its mixture of delicious flavours is very popular.

Let's put it together now!

This student has left out two words and five commas in this section of his recount on Italian food. Use a red pen to fill in the words and **commas** for him.

Italian food with its rich flavours and fresh ingredients is enjoyed by men women and children all over the world. The most popular foods from Italy are pasta pizza and different types of cheeses. Customers Italian restaurants usually order pasta or pizza. Italian restaurants also serve lots gelato. Of all the different types of food I like Italian food the best!

Let's have fun!

1. Match the noun in Column 1 with the **adjectival phrase** that tells more about it in Column 2. Shade the matching pairs the same colour. The first pair has been done for you.

Noun	Adjectival phrase
the flavours	on the barbecue
chefs	from the freezer
lettuce	with cream topping
pizza	of Tom Yum Soup
gelato	from France
dessert	on a salad sandwich
sausages	in the wood-fired oven

2. Help the chef complete these dishes by sprinkling on the **commas**. Make sure they land in the right places!

To complete this dish I still need to add the herbs adjust the seasoning and heat it through.

I will finish off the dessert with a swirl of cream shaved chocolate nuts and a cherry.

Let's have a test!

1 Which sentence has been written correctly?

- ◯ A chef of a famous restaurant is preparing our meal.
- ◯ A chef by a famous restaurant is preparing our meal.
- ◯ A chef from a famous restaurant is preparing our meal.
- ◯ A chef on a famous restaurant is preparing our meal.

In questions 2–3, choose the words that complete the sentence correctly.

2 The dish ________________ in it is very spicy.

◯ has chillies ◯ with chillies ◯ of chillies ◯ have chillies

3 I ordered steak ________________.

◯ without sauce ◯ from sauce ◯ has sauce ◯ have sauce

4 Which words do **not** complete this sentence correctly?

The doughnuts ________________ are delicious!

◯ from the bakery ◯ at the bakery ◯ on the bakery ◯ in the bakery

5 Which list has been written correctly?

- ◯ a pie, mashed, potatoes and gravy
- ◯ a pie, mashed, potatoes, and gravy
- ◯ a pie, mashed potatoes, and gravy
- ◯ a pie, mashed potatoes and gravy

In questions 6–7, choose where the comma should go.

6 I like Italian ◯ food ◯ Chinese ◯ food ◯ and Mexican food.

7 I like many Mexican ◯ dishes ◯ especially ◯ the very ◯ spicy ones.

8 Which sentence has been punctuated correctly?

- ◯ In some countries such as China, Korea and Japan, people use chopsticks.
- ◯ In some countries, such as China, Korea and Japan, people use chopsticks.
- ◯ In some countries, such as China, Korea, and Japan, people use chopsticks.
- ◯ In some countries, such as China, Korea and Japan people use chopsticks.

Let's write now!

Answer one of the following.

1. Write a **recount** about a time you went to a restaurant that serves food from another country. Tell what you ordered and what it tasted like.
2. Find a **recipe** for a dish from a foreign country and write it out, using the example text as a model. Use **adjectival phrases** and **commas** in your recipe.

Unit 9 Safety rules!

Focus
Sentences: statements and questions; commands and exclamations

Safety in the home

by Francine

This is a **comic strip**. A comic strip tells stories or gives information. Francine's characters use **statements** to give information and **questions** to ask for information in this conversation between Claire and her mum.

Sentences
- are groups of words that make sense when they stand on their own.
- always contain a verb; for example, **Your little brother <u>puts</u> everything in his mouth.**
- are used to tell a story or anything else we want to write about.

Questions
- are sentences that ask for information.
- always start with a capital letter and end with a question mark.

For example: **<u>W</u>hy are you putting away my coins, Mum<u>?</u>**

Statements
- are sentences that give information.
- always start with a capital letter and end with a full stop.

For example: **<u>I</u> was counting them<u>.</u>**

Let's find them!

Write down whether these **sentences** from the text are **questions** or **statements**.

1. I was counting them. ____________________
2. Do you want him to choke? ____________________

3. Would he put these beads in his mouth? ____________

4. They're very colourful. ____________

5. What do you think? ____________

6. I'd better keep them out of his reach. ____________

7. What else can I do to keep the house safe for Sammy, Mum? ____________

Let's go to the next step!

Find the **statement** that answers each **question** and shade the matching pairs the same colour. The first pair has been done for you.

Questions	Statements
1 How did you know there was a fire?	I moved it away from the heater.
2 What's wrong with your finger?	You should learn how to swim.
3 Why are you washing your hands?	I won't let you stay at home alone.
4 Where is that pile of old newspapers?	I cut it while I was chopping the carrots.
5 Do I have to go with you to the shops?	He's going to use the leaf blower.
6 How can I be safe in the water?	The smoke alarm went off.
7 Why is Dad wearing earmuffs?	I don't want to spread germs and diseases.

Let's aim high now!

Change these **statements** into **questions** by starting each sentence with the verb.
For example:
There are lots of safety hints on the Internet. *Are there lots of safety hints on the Internet?*

1. The girl has had a bad accident. ____________

2. Roller skates can be dangerous. ____________

3. She will be more careful in future. ____________

4. She is teaching him how to swim. ____________

5. He has worn safety glasses before. ____________

6. The cyclists were putting on their helmets. ____________

7. He should change the battery in the fire alarm. ____________

Reckless Roderick

by Toby

This is another **comic strip**. Toby's characters use **commands** to tell Reckless Roderick what he should be doing, and **exclamations** to express strong feelings while pointing out some important safety rules.

Commands

- are sentences that tell someone to do something, or give an order.
- start with a verb.
- end with a full stop or exclamation mark.

For example: **Cross at the pedestrian crossing.**

Exclamations

- are sentences that express strong emotions or feelings.
- always end with an exclamation mark (!).

For example: **How dangerous is that!**

Let's find them!

Write down whether these **sentences** from the text are **commands** or **exclamations**.

1. Ride your skateboard at the skate park! ________________
2. I don't believe it! ________________
3. Put on your helmet. ________________
4. He just won't listen! ________________
5. Wait for the traffic light to change! ________________
6. That's asking for trouble! ________________
7. Keep out of there! ________________

Let's go to the next step!

Complete each **command** with a verb from the box. Use each verb once.

Keep	Wear	Drive	Throw	Hold	Switch	Stay

1. ________________ that banana skin in the bin.
2. ________________ off the heater when you go to bed.
3. ________________ a hat if you're going to sit in the sun.
4. "________________ away from that building site," ordered Dad.
5. ________________ onto the rail when you walk down the stairs.
6. ________________ your dog on a leash when you take it for a walk.
7. "________________ carefully," Mum said to Dad as they got into the car.

Tip!
Read through all of the sentences before deciding which verbs to use.

Let's aim high now!

Which emotion or feeling is each of these speakers expressing? Choose a word from the box and write it in the space next to the **sentence**. Use each word once.

anger	delight	admiration	pain	disbelief	sympathy	disgust

1. "Ouch, that knife is sharp!" howled Joe. ________________
2. "Oh, you poor girl!" exclaimed the teacher. ________________
3. "How could you be so reckless!" yelled Mum. ________________
4. "What an ugly fire hydrant!" boomed the old lady. ________________
5. "I've never seen flooding like this before!" he exclaimed. ________________
6. "Hooray, I finished the skipping race without tripping!" whooped Julia. ________________
7. "What a magnificent advertisement for road safety!" beamed the man. ________________

Let's put it together now!

This student has used the wrong **punctuation** in his comic strip. Use a red pen to make the corrections for him.

Let's have fun!

Look at the **sentences** in the box. Decide who says what in this comic strip, and then draw the correct number of speech bubbles. Write the sentences in the bubbles.

Have you cleaned up yet?	I'm doing it now, Mum.
What a mess!	Be careful!

Let's have a test!

In questions 1–2, which sentence has been written correctly?

1
- ◯ That ride is dangerous.
- ◯ Is that ride dangerous.
- ◯ Why is that ride dangerous.
- ◯ Will you go on that dangerous ride.

2
- ◯ He has fallen many times?
- ◯ How many times has he fallen?
- ◯ He is always falling?
- ◯ He falls a lot?

3 Which word completes this sentence correctly?

________ he try that difficult jump?

◯ Why ◯ How ◯ Should ◯ Shall

4 Which word does **not** complete this sentence correctly?

________ is he going to climb that cliff?

◯ Why ◯ What ◯ When ◯ How

5 In which sentence is Mike's dad giving an order?

- ◯ Building sites are dangerous.
- ◯ Is the building site dangerous?
- ◯ That building site is dangerous.
- ◯ Keep away from the building site!

6 Which word completes this sentence correctly?

________ amazing that he did not hurt himself!

◯ What ◯ How ◯ It ◯ That

7 Which word does **not** complete this sentence correctly?

________ at the pedestrian crossing.

◯ Cross ◯ Wait ◯ Stop ◯ Go

8 Which sentence shows that Min is scared of the dog?

- ◯ That dog has very big teeth.
- ◯ Does that dog have big teeth?
- ◯ That dog has very big teeth!
- ◯ Some dogs have very big teeth!

Let's write now!

Think of a situation in which we need to follow safety rules, such as when we are in a forest or at the beach, and create a **comic strip** to express your message. Let your characters use **statements**, **questions**, **commands** and **exclamations**. Model your comic strip on the texts in this unit.

Unit 10 Digging up the past

Focus
Simple sentences; clauses and compound sentences; conjunctions; commas

Finding Pompeii

Archeologists study the past. They excavate and examine the remains of ancient sites.

Pompeii in Italy is one of the most famous archeological sites in the world. Nearly 2000 years ago, it was buried beneath a pile of ash and debris when Mount Vesuvius erupted. Excavations on the site started about 250 years ago. They continue to this day. By digging up Pompeii, archeologists have been able to piece together evidence to give us a good idea of what life was like in Italy 2000 years ago. Volcanic ash covered the city very quickly, so everything in it was well preserved. Archeologists discovered the outlines of 2000 bodies. They also found bread in an oven!

Artifacts from the Pompeii dig are exhibited in museums around the world. Pompeii is one of Italy's most popular tourist destinations. More than two million people visit it every year!

This is an **article** from a magazine. The main purpose of a magazine article is to entertain and inform. The author uses **simple sentences** containing subjects and predicates while informing us about the archeological site at Pompeii.

Simple sentences

- are groups of words that contain complete ideas or messages.
- have a subject—the person, place or thing that the sentence is about.
- have a predicate—the rest of the sentence that contains the verb or verb group, and gives more information about the subject.

For example: **Archeologists study the past.** In this sentence, the subject is *Archeologists*, the predicate is *study the past* and the verb is *study*.

Rule!

Subjects must agree with their verbs; for example:

- **An archeologist studies the past.**
- **Archeologists study the past.**

Let's find them!

Underline the **subjects** and circle the **verbs** in these **simple sentences** from the text.

1. Pompeii in Italy is one of the most famous archeological sites in the world.
2. Excavations on the site started about 250 years ago.
3. They continue to this day.

4. Archeologists discovered the outlines of 2000 bodies.
5. They also found bread in an oven!
6. Pompeii is one of Italy's most popular tourist destinations.
7. More than two million people visit it every year!

Tip!

The subject of a sentence can be more than one word; for example, Artifacts from the Pompeii dig are exhibited in museums around the world.

Let's go to the next step!

Choose the correct **verb** or **verb group** in brackets to complete each **simple sentence**. Cross out the incorrect one.

For example: We (go/~~goes~~) to archeological digs all the time.

1. My friend (have been/has been) to Pompeii before.
2. I (am learning/are learning) about archeological digs.
3. Their cousins (have been/has been) to Pompeii lots of times.
4. A farmer in England (is finding/are finding) old coins in his fields.
5. The archeologists from the dig (is eating/are eating) their dinner.
6. She (was looking/were looking) for information on archeological digs.
7. The people at the dig (was watching/were watching) the archeologist.

Let's aim high now!

Match the **subject** in the first column with its **predicate** in the second column. Shade the matching pairs the same colour.

Subjects	Predicates
1 Artifacts from Pompeii	was about the destruction of Pompeii.
2 The archeologist	is a fascinating place.
3 Everyone on the dig	include frescoes, coins and statues.
4 The tourists	contain pictures of archeological digs.
5 The documentary	is working on a new dig.
6 The books in the library	shares the archeologist's enthusiasm.
7 The archeological dig	were looking forward to their visit to Pompeii.

The terracotta warriors

In 1974, some farmers in China found a number of clay statues in a field. They reported their find to the authorities and archeologists were soon excavating the site. They found a whole army of clay figures! What is so amazing about them? **Thousands of statues have been unearthed, yet no two are alike.** The statues are life-sized and they are life-like. Some are marching and others are kneeling. The list goes on.

The statues form part of the tomb of the first emperor of China and are in underground trenches. In some of the trenches there are clay horses with wooden chariots behind them. Archeologists have even found swords and other weapons in some trenches.

This is another magazine **article**. The author uses **conjunctions** when joining **simple sentences** to make **compound sentences** while informing us about the terracotta warriors in China.

Clauses
- are groups of words that contain a complete idea or message.
- contain a verb or verb group; for example, **In 1974, some farmers in China found a number of clay statues in a field.**

Main clauses contain the main idea or message.

Simple sentences have one main clause.

Compound sentences have two or more main clauses joined by a **conjunction**; for example, **They reported their find to the authorities and archeologists were soon excavating the site**.

Rule!

Conjunctions are joining words.
- They join single words or phrases in sentences; for example, **authorities and archeologists**.
- They also join **simple sentences** to make **compound sentences**; for example, **Thousands of statues have been unearthed, yet no two are alike.**

Let's find them!

Underline the **verbs** or **verb groups** in these sentences from the text and state whether they are **simple** or **compound sentences**.

For example: The archeologists found a whole army of clay figures! simple sentence

Tip!
Conjunctions include the words **and**, **but**, **or**, **so** and **yet**.

1. Thousands of statues have been unearthed, yet no two are alike. ______
2. Some are marching and others are kneeling. ______
3. The list goes on. ______
4. The statues form part of the tomb of the first emperor of China and are in underground trenches. ______

5 In some of the trenches there are clay horses with wooden chariots behind them. ____________________

6 Archeologists have found swords and other weapons in some trenches. ____________________

Tip!
Remember: if there is one verb, it is a **simple sentence**; if there is more than one verb, it is a **compound sentence**.

Let's go to the next step!

Complete these **compound sentences** with a **clause** from the box.

but some escaped	and they died instantly
but I haven't seen the terracotta warriors	so she organised a visit to a dig
yet she got lost	so it is still a threat
or she might be in the museum	

1 The molten ash covered the people ____________________.

2 The archeologist knew the area well, ____________________.

3 Many of the residents of Pompeii were killed, ____________________.

4 Mount Vesuvius could erupt at any time, ____________________.

5 The archeologist might be at the dig, ____________________.

6 I have seen Pompeii, ____________________.

7 My mother is interested in archeology, ____________________.

Tip!
A **comma** usually separates clauses that are joined by **yet**, **but**, **or** and **so**.

Let's aim high now!

Use the conjunctions *and*, *but*, *or*, *so* or *yet* to join these **clauses** to make **compound sentences**.

Rule!
When joining more than two **simple sentences** to form a **compound sentence**, we normally use a **comma** and a **conjunction**; for example:
I found the old jar. Tom repaired it. Jenny painted it.
I found the old jar, Tom repaired it and Jenny painted it.

1 He is an archeologist, ______________ he has never worked on a dig.

2 The bus was going to Pompeii, ______________ the tourists climbed aboard.

3 The children found some coins in the field, ______________ they weren't very old.

4 The shards of pottery are the same colour, ______________ they don't belong together.

5 They might be a dinosaur's bones, ______________ they might be a mammoth's bones.

6 I went to an archeological site he went to a museum ______________ she visited the caves.

7 The statue was made of marble the jar was made of clay ______________ the plate was made of silver.

Let's put it together now!

This student has left out three **conjunctions** and three **commas** in her article about Stonehenge. There is also a verb that doesn't agree with its subject. Use a red pen to insert or correct the conjunctions, fill in the missing punctuation and correct the verb.

Stonehenge in England are almost 5000 years old. Archeologists have studied the site they have dug up artifacts they have unearthed an ancient village nearby. But Stonehenge's past remains a mystery. Experts do have some ideas about what Stonehenge may have been used for. Ancient people may have used it as an observatory it may have been a cemetery. Archeologists are still searching for answers to Stonehenge's past they are no closer to finding them.

Let's have fun!

Join the words on these chain links to form a **simple sentence** of six words. Two of the words do not belong in the sentence and should be crossed out.

Write the simple sentence here:

Now join these words to form a **compound sentence** containing nine words. Three of the words do not belong in the sentence and should be crossed out.

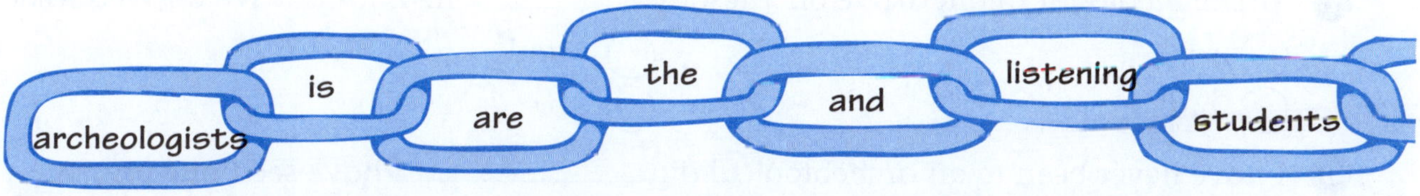

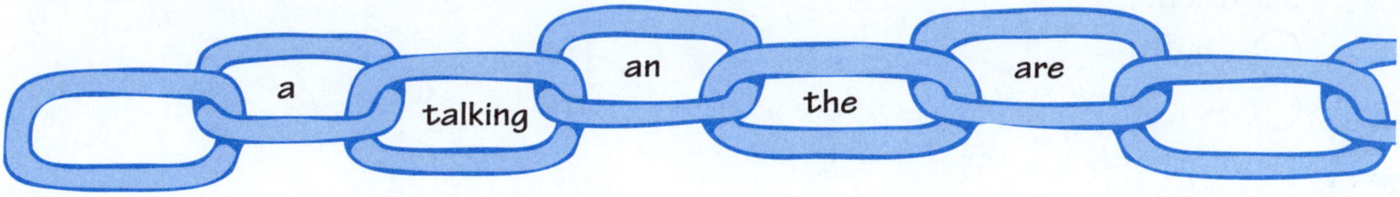

Write the compound sentence here:

Let's have a test!

In questions 1–6, which words complete the sentence correctly?

1 __________ are in the museum.

- ○ The pot
- ○ The statues
- ○ A jewel
- ○ An archeologist

2 __________ were about Pompeii.

- ○ The film
- ○ A program
- ○ An article
- ○ The books

3 The archeologist __________ the coins.

- ○ are counting
- ○ am counting
- ○ is counting
- ○ count

4 The students __________ the archeologist.

- ○ was helping
- ○ are helping
- ○ is helping
- ○ helps

5 I went to the museum __________ I saw the famous statue.

- ○ but
- ○ and
- ○ or
- ○ yet

6 You can read about the dig, __________ you can visit it.

- ○ but
- ○ yet
- ○ so
- ○ or

In questions 7–8, which words and punctuation complete the sentence correctly?

7 The archeologist might arrive on Tuesday __________ he might arrive on Wednesday.

- ○ so,
- ○ but,
- ○ , and
- ○ , or

8 I have never been to an archeological dig __________ I have seen one on television.

- ○ , but
- ○ yet,
- ○ , or
- ○ and,

Let's write now!

Look in books or on the Internet for information on famous archeological sites. Write an **article** for your school magazine on the archeological site you have chosen. Use **simple** and **compound sentences** in your article.

Unit 11 Insects with dirty habits

Focus
Complex sentences; conjunctions; relative pronouns; dependent clauses; commas

Dung beetles

Dung beetles love the waste that other animals produce. They eat it, live in it and reproduce in it.

Dung beetles are found on all continents except Antarctica. Although they eat the waste matter of many different animals, they prefer the dung of herbivores. They don't need to eat or drink anything else, as they get all their nutrients from the dung.

Once beetles have found dung, they roll it away in a straight line. When they come to an obstacle, they just keep going. If the ball of dung rolls back down a rise, the beetle just rolls it back up again.

Dung beetles are actually much stronger than humans. They can roll a ball of dung that is ten times their weight. That's like you or me trying to push something which weighs about 320 kg!

By burying and eating dung, these little creatures help to improve the soil, so many countries have introduced them into their ecosystems.

by Chris

This is an **information report**. An information report gives factual information about people, animals or things. Chris uses **complex sentences** to give factual information about the dung beetle.

In Unit 10 you learnt that a simple sentence has one main clause and a compound sentence has two main clauses.

Complex sentences have
- one main clause that contains the main idea or message of the sentence.
- at least one other clause that contains a verb but cannot stand on its own.

For example: **Dung beetles love the waste <u>that other animals produce.</u>**

Dependent clauses can be introduced by a
- **conjunction**; for example, after, although, as, because, before, if, once, since, so, though, unless, until, when, whenever, where, whereas, wherever, whether, while.
- **relative pronoun**; for example, that, which, who, whom, whose.

Let's find them!

Underline the **conjunctions** and **relative pronouns** that introduce **dependent clauses** in the text. Be careful! Some dependent clauses come at the beginning of the sentence! Write them on the next page.

1 ______________________ 5 ______________________

2 ______________________ 6 ______________________

3 ______________________ 7 ______________________

4 ______________________ 8 ______________________

Let's go to the next step!

Underline the **dependent clause** in these sentences.
For example: I watched the dung beetle until it got dark.

1. The flies won't get onto the meat if you cover it.
2. When we went to China, we saw lots of dried dung beetles.
3. I've learnt a lot about dung beetles since I last saw you.
4. I watched in fascination as the dung beetle rolled its ball of dung over the anthill.
5. Dung beetles are sometimes called rollers because they roll dung into balls.
6. The scarab beetle, which is a type of dung beetle, was once thought to be sacred.
7. Our soil will continue to deteriorate, unless we bring more dung beetles into the country.

Let's aim high now!

Make **complex sentences** by matching the **main** and **dependent clauses** in the columns. Shade the matching pairs the same colour.

Main clauses	Dependent clauses
1 There are lots of scientists in the world	until it got the dung ball over the rise.
2 I became interested in dung beetles	where we saw images of scarab beetles.
3 We went to a temple in Egypt	after I'd handled the dung ball.
4 I'd never seen a real one until today.	who study dung beetles.
5 Mum made me wash my hands	Wherever we went on the farm,
6 we saw dung beetles.	when I saw one in our garden
7 The dung beetle kept on trying	Although I'd seen many pictures of dung beetles,

Cockroaches

Cockroaches, which are found all over the world, are pests. They eat our food and carry germs. They can also leave a bad smell in the house.

It isn't easy to get rid of cockroaches. They can survive for long periods without food, water or air. After being submerged in water for half an hour, they are able to recover. Some experts even say that if there's a nuclear explosion, cockroaches will survive. And although they prefer warm climates, they can live in freezing temperatures.

Cockroaches are mainly nocturnal. When exposed to light, they run away. This also makes it difficult to get rid of them, as they are so hard to find. An exception is the Asian cockroach, which is attracted to light.

Because cockroaches are a danger to our health, we should try to keep them out of our homes.

by Stella

This is another **information report**. Stella uses **commas** to separate clauses while giving us information about cockroaches.

So far you have learnt that **commas** are used

- to separate nouns, adjectives and actions in a list.
- to separate phrases from the rest of the sentence.
- before certain conjunctions in compound sentences.

Commas are also used to separate **clauses** in **complex sentences**; for example, **Cockroaches, which are found all over the world, are pests.**

Let's find them!

Find these sentences in the text and fill in the **commas** that separate the **dependent clauses** from the rest of the sentence.

1. After being submerged in water for half an hour they are able to recover.
2. Some experts even say that if there is a nuclear explosion cockroaches will survive.
3. And although they prefer warm climates they can live in freezing temperatures.
4. When exposed to light they run away.
5. This also makes it difficult to get rid of them as they are so hard to find.
6. An exception is the Asian cockroach which is attracted to light.
7. Because cockroaches are a danger to our health we should try to keep them out of our homes.

Let's go to the next step!

Fill in **commas** to separate the **dependent clauses** from the rest of the sentence. Be careful—some dependent clauses come in the middle of the sentence!

1. When I looked in the box I saw two cockroaches.
2. Although I can't see the cockroach I know it's there.
3. While you search for the cockroach I'll empty the bins.
4. If you don't want cockroaches eating your food cover it.
5. The cockroach which was enormous was staring at me.
6. Whenever my little sister sees a cockroach she screams.
7. The scientist who has spent years studying cockroaches will retire soon.

Let's aim high now!

Complete each sentence with a **dependent clause** from the box. Don't forget the **commas**!

Before we moved into the house	mainly because they can spread diseases
When they checked out of the hotel	which is found in Australia
While dung beetles help humans	whose mum works with mine
Although I hear cockroaches	

1. ________________________________ I never see them.
2. The boy ________________________________ collects cockroaches!
3. ________________________________ we checked for cockroaches.
4. The world's biggest cockroach ________________________________ is 9 cm long.
5. ________________________________ cockroaches are of no use to them.
6. I don't like cockroaches ________________________________.
7. ________________________________ they complained about the cockroaches.

Let's put it together now!

This student has left out seven **commas** in his information report about flies. Use a red pen to fill them in.

Wherever there are people there are flies. The house fly which makes up about 90% of all domestic flies is the most widely distributed of all insects. Because it can carry serious diseases it is considered a pest. The female lays about 500 eggs and within a day, the larvae, known as maggots, hatch. After they have gorged themselves on dead and decaying matter they become pupae. The adult flies emerge from the pupae. Adult flies which are 8–12 mm long live for between two weeks and a month.

Let's have fun!

Find these words in the wordsearch puzzle. The words go forwards, backwards, up and down.

as	fly	if	until	dung
when	after	unless	that	since
	where	cockroach	who	

n	e	v	s	s	e	l	n	u	b	m	i
w	c	h	g	r	q	x	b	d	y	o	p
a	n	f	c	o	c	k	r	o	a	c	h
t	i	v	e	j	k	q	b	n	r	q	c
c	s	r	t	a	h	t	u	w	a	b	x
i	v	r	s	w	t	k	a	f	t	e	r
f	p	n	m	s	a	z	z	w	q	g	y
w	c	e	o	x	g	e	r	u	y	l	f
d	b	h	q	b	e	r	q	x	b	s	z
u	e	w	o	v	y	e	b	d	m	v	s
n	t	t	y	q	p	h	u	n	t	i	l
g	i	o	h	w	a	w	n	q	w	x	z

Let's have a test!

1. Which sentence has been written correctly?
   - ◯ The girl, who father is an entomologist, knows a lot about insects
   - ◯ The girl, whose father is an entomologist, knows a lot about insects.
   - ◯ The girl, whom father is an entomologist, knows a lot about insects.
   - ◯ The girl, which father is an entomologist, knows a lot about insects.

In questions 2–4, which word completes the sentence correctly?

2. This is the same fly ________ was in the kitchen earlier.
   - ◯ who ◯ what ◯ it ◯ that

3. I saw the cockroach ________ I was looking for a plate.
   - ◯ while ◯ after ◯ although ◯ until

4. There are no flies in our house ________ we have screens on the windows.
   - ◯ when ◯ because ◯ unless ◯ where

In questions 5–6, show where the comma(s) go in the sentence.

5. Although ◯ cockroaches ◯ are pests ◯ I am not ◯ frightened of them.

6. The dung beetle ◯ which was burying ◯ its dung ◯ was attacked ◯ by a bird.

In questions 7–8, which word and punctuation completes the sentence correctly?

7. I don't like dung beetles ________ he loves them!
   - ◯ , whenever ◯ whereas,
   - ◯ , whereas ◯ , whether

8. The dung beetle ________ was crossing the road, was rolling a dung ball.
   - ◯ , which ◯ which,
   - ◯ , who ◯ who,

Let's write now!

Look in books or on the Internet for information on unusual insects, especially those with dirty habits! Write an **information report** on the insect you have chosen. Use **complex sentences** and **commas** to separate clauses in your report.

Unit 12 Strange, but true

Focus
Adjectival clauses; noun groups

Bad timing!

A crocodile at a zoo in Russia has gone off its food since swallowing a zookeeper's mobile phone.

The zookeeper, **who was taking a photograph of the reptile**, accidentally dropped her phone. The croc, whose mouth was open, caught and swallowed it. Now the crocodile, which used to have an excellent appetite, has stopped eating. The phone, which continues to respond to calls, is stuck somewhere in the croc's stomach. Vets, who have been monitoring the croc since the accident, say that the phone will have to be removed surgically. Crocs, which are cranky at the best of times, get even crankier when they are in pain. Neither the vets nor the zookeepers are looking forward to the operation!

This is a **newspaper report**. A newspaper report informs readers about events around the world. The reporter uses **adjectival clauses** to give more information about people, animals, places or things in this report about a crocodile that swallowed a mobile phone.

Adjectival clauses are dependent clauses that
- give more information about people, animals, places or things.
- are usually introduced by the relative pronouns *who, whose, whom, which* or *that.*

For example: **who was taking a photograph of the reptile** gives more information about the zookeeper.

Let's find them!

Find these **adjectival clauses** in the text and write down who or what they give more information about.

1. whose mouth was open ____________
2. which used to have an excellent appetite ____________
3. which continues to respond to calls ____________
4. who have been monitoring the croc since the accident ____________
5. which are cranky at the best of times ____________

Let's go to the next step!

Complete the **adjectival clauses** in these sentences with a relative pronoun.

1. The dentist ____________ I go to has false teeth!
2. The boy, ____________ is only five years old, can walk on his hands!
3. The humming bird is the only bird ____________ can fly backwards.
4. This is the woman ____________ has the longest fingernails in the world.
5. The crocodile, ____________ teeth fall out regularly, is able to grow new ones.
6. Venus, ____________ is the second planet from the sun, spins from east to west.
7. The Great Pyramid of Giza, ____________ is in Egypt, is thousands of years old.

Let's aim high now!

Tip! Read through all of the sentences before filling in the clauses.

Complete these sentences with an **adjectival clause** from the box. Use each clause once.

which is a crowded city	whose favourite food is meat
who sits next to me	that I read in a science magazine
that my brother caught	which had been missing for four years
whom I interviewed	

1. The octopus ________________________ has blue blood!
2. The scientist ________________________ knows a lot about black holes.
3. A cat, ________________________, is unable to taste sweetness.
4. The boy ________________________ once hiccupped through an entire lesson!
5. In Tokyo, ________________________, lots of people ride bicycles.
6. Our neighbour's cat, ________________________ came home last week.
7. The article ________________________ contained interesting facts.

In a tight spot

A would-be burglar found himself in a tight spot last night when he got stuck in a window.

The **tall, thin burglar** was attempting to enter a house through a small, unlocked window downstairs. When he was halfway through, he became stuck. His only option was to wait for someone to rescue him. He spent an uncomfortable six hours before the owner came downstairs and found him. The owner immediately notified the police. Although they tried for almost an hour, they were unable to free the man. They called in the help of the fire department, who used bolt cutters to cut him loose. The burglar, who was not allowed to speak to us, was led away in handcuffs.

The owner of the house said he never locked the window because he thought it was too small for a burglar to fit through.

This is another **newspaper report**. The reporter uses **noun groups** to give more information about the people, places and things involved in this report about a burglar who found himself in a tight spot.

Noun groups are groups of words that are built around nouns. They give more information about the people, places and things being written about.

Noun groups can include

- the articles *a*, *an* or *the*; for example, a burglar.
- a pronoun; for example, that burglar.
- one or more adjectives; for example, the **tall, thin burglar**.
- an adjectival phrase; for example, the tall, thin burglar in the window.
- an adjectival clause; for example, the tall, thin burglar who got stuck in a window.

Let's find them!

Underline the nouns around which these **noun groups** from the text have been built. The first one has been done for you.

1. a tight spot
2. a small, unlocked window
3. His only option
4. an uncomfortable six hours
5. the help of the fire department

6 The burglar, who was not allowed to speak to us,

7 The owner of the house

Let's go to the next step!

Tip! Some sentences have more than one **noun group**.

Underline the **noun groups** in these sentences.
For example: That was the strangest story I had ever heard.

1 I read the story about the burglar yesterday.

2 The pizza, which was huge, fed fifty people!

3 My brother's dog has short legs and a long tail.

4 The old lady, who loves animals, has sixteen cats!

5 The little girl in the pink dress can juggle five balls!

6 I saw a cockroach without a head running across the room.

7 Some spectators at the cricket match were wearing strange outfits.

Let's aim high now!

Complete these sentences with a **noun group** from the box.

a python that is six metres long	its own strange stories
Sneezing with your eyes open	The shop, which has just opened,
The burglar who got stuck in the window	your heart
a book about strange events	

1 Did you know that ______________________________
stops when you sneeze?

2 The man has written ______________________________.

3 ______________________________ is impossible.

4 Every country has ______________________________.

5 ______________________________ was arrested.

6 At the zoo there is ______________________________.

7 ______________________________, sells shoes.

Let's put it together now!

This student has left out the following words in his report. Can you fill them in for him?

who	your	that	whose	poor	a	which

Some people have names ______________ cause them problems. ______________ Stan Still doesn't know what to do when people say, "Stan Still! Get a move on!"

A website, ___________ recently conducted a survey of people's names, found that many parents don't think of the problems that unusual names could cause for their children. There are people ___________ parents have named them Chris when their surname is Cross, and Paige when their surname is Turner. And then there's Mr Hole, ___________ is stuck with the name Doug. ___________ spokesperson for the website said, "Think before you choose a name for ___________ child. If your surname is Case, don't call your child Justin or Justine."

Let's have fun!

Complete these puzzles by filling in pairs of words from the lists below. Fit the **relative pronouns** and **adjectives** into the blocks going across, and the **nouns** into the blocks going down. The first one has been done for you.

Across: (relative pronouns and adjectives) whom, cranky, whose, which, funny, that, who, tall

Down: (nouns) boy, name, chimp, crocodile, farm, person, burglar, woman

Let's have a test!

1 Which sentence has been written correctly?

- ◯ This strange story which comes from Spain.
- ◯ This story, which comes from Spain, is strange.
- ◯ This story from Spain which is strange.
- ◯ This story, which is strange, from Spain.

2 Which underlined word can be left out of this sentence without changing the meaning?

We listened to the story which was strange, but was true.

◯ to ◯ which ◯ but ◯ was

In questions 3–6, show which option completes the sentence correctly.

3 That's the teacher ____________.

- ◯ what told us the story
- ◯ whose told us the story
- ◯ which told us the story
- ◯ who told us the story

4 The bird ____________ is a humming bird.

- ◯ that is flying backwards
- ◯ who is flying backwards
- ◯ whom is flying backwards
- ◯ whose is flying backwards

5 He saw ____________ burglar stuck in a window.

- ◯ an tall, thin
- ◯ those tall thin
- ◯ a tall, thin
- ◯ tall, thin

6 ____________ were lying on the river bank.

- ◯ A very big crocodile
- ◯ Two very big crocodiles
- ◯ Very big crocodile
- ◯ The very big crocodile

In questions 7–8, choose the words that do **not** complete the sentence correctly.

7 The burglar will not fit through ____________.

- ◯ such a small window
- ◯ an small window
- ◯ that small window
- ◯ the small window

8 ____________ dropped her mobile phone.

- ◯ An experienced zookeeper
- ◯ That experienced zookeeper
- ◯ The experienced zookeeper
- ◯ A experienced zookeeper

Let's write now!

Think of a story that is strange, but could be true, and write it as a **newspaper report**. Use **noun groups** containing **adjectival clauses** in your report.

Unit 13 Australian artists

Focus

Adverbial clauses; brackets; colons; ellipses

Albert Namatjira

Albert Namatjira, a member of the Western Aranda tribe, is one of Australia's best-known artists. He learnt skills such as carpentry and sheep shearing **while he lived on a mission station in the Northern Territory**. However, after studying the works of the artists Rex Battarbee and John Gardner, Albert started painting his own landscapes. When Battarbee saw Albert's talent, he offered to give him lessons.

Albert held his first exhibition in Melbourne in 1938. People loved his landscapes, and he soon gained international recognition. He was awarded the Queen's Coronation Medal in 1953 and was presented to Queen Elizabeth when she came to Australia the following year.

Although Albert died in 1959, his paintings remain popular.

by Jayden

This is a **biography**. A biography is an account of someone's life written by someone else. Jayden uses **adverbial clauses** to give more information about verbs in his biography of Albert Namatjira.

Adverbial clauses are dependent clauses that give more information about verbs; for example, **while he lived on a mission station in the Northern Territory** gives more information about where he learnt the skills.

They are usually introduced by a conjunction; for example, **while he lived on a mission station in the Northern Territory**.

Some of the conjunctions that introduce dependent clauses are:
after, although, as, because, before, if, once, since, though, unless, until, when.

Let's find them!

Underline the **adverbial clauses** in these sentences from the text.

1. He learnt skills such as carpentry and sheep shearing while he lived on a mission station.
2. However, after studying the works of the artists Rex Battarbee and John Gardner, Albert started painting his own landscapes.

3. When Battarbee saw Albert's talent, he offered to give him lessons.
4. He was awarded the Queen's Coronation Medal in 1953 and was presented to Queen Elizabeth when she came to Australia the following year.
5. Although Albert died in 1959, his paintings remain popular.

Let's go to the next step!

Complete the **adverbial clauses** in these sentences with a conjunction from the box. Use each word once.

because if unless whenever although since until

1. ________________ you go to the art gallery, you will see Albert Namatjira's work.
2. It's been more than fifty years ________________ Albert Namatjira died.
3. She'd never heard of Albert Namatjira ________________ I told her about him.
4. ________________ Albert Namatjira held an exhibition, he sold many paintings.
5. People bought Albert Namatjira's paintings ________________ they liked them.
6. ________________ I've never seen any of his paintings, I know they are very good.
7. You don't have to go to the art gallery, ________________ you want to see a particular painting.

Let's aim high now!

Find the **main** and **adverbial clauses** that go together and shade the matching pairs the same colour. The first one has been done for you.

Main clause	Adverbial clause
1 it isn't for sale.	once we've seen all the paintings.
2 I knew who the artist was.	When we get to the art gallery,
3 The artist takes her sketchpad with her	because they are very dull.
4 We'll stay at the art gallery	Although I'd like to buy the painting,
5 you can look at whatever you wish.	until it closes.
6 I don't like those paintings	As soon as I saw the painting,
7 We'll go to the café	wherever she goes.

Interviewing Margaret Olley

Margaret Olley **(1923–2011)** was an Australian artist best known for her still-life paintings. This is an imaginary interview with her.

Alison: What made you become an artist?

Margaret: **Mmm … I'm not really sure …** except that I lived for art lessons at school.

Alison: Did anyone encourage you to become an artist?

Margaret: (without hesitation) My mother!

Alison: In what way did she encourage you?

Margaret: Well … I suppose she encouraged me to be what I wanted to be. **Her motto was: "If you want to do something, do it!"**

Alison: Where do you find inspiration for your paintings?

Margaret: I paint what's around me (gesturing at the objects in the room). It's easier that way.

by Alison

This is an **interview**. An interview is a conversation between two people in which one person asks questions to get information from the other person. Alison uses **brackets**, **colons** and **ellipses** to punctuate her imaginary interview with Margaret Olley.

Brackets go around words or numbers that add information to the text; for example, **(1923–2011)** tells when Margaret Olley was born and when she died.

Colons (:) are used
- after the speaker's name in a script or interview; for example, **Alison:**
- to show that more information is to follow; for example, **Her motto was: "If you want to do something, do it!"**

Ellipses (singular: **ellipsis**) consist of three dots (**…**). They show a pause in speech; for example, **Mmm … I'm not really sure** …

Let's find them!

Underline the words in **brackets**, put a circle around the **colons** and put boxes around the **ellipses** in these phrases and sentences from the text.

1. I'm not really sure … except
2. Alison: Did anyone encourage you to become an artist?

3. Margaret: (without hesitation) My mother!
4. Well … I suppose
5. Her motto was: "If you want to do something, do it!"
6. I paint what's around me (gesturing at the objects in the room).

Let's go to the next step!

The **brackets**, **colons** and **ellipses** in these sentences are in the wrong place. Use a red pen to show where they should be.
For example: The artist: used these colours purple, red, green and brown.

1. I was thinking no, that … wouldn't work.
2. (Pablo Picasso) 1881–1973 is a very famous artist.
3. Let's see you could paint … those hills a lighter colour.
4. I've visited: galleries on many continents Europe, America and Australia.
5. Albert Namatjira was born on a mission station in the (Northern Territory) NT.
6. The artist has collected: many objects old tyres, bits of steel and balls of string.
7. Which of these canvases: should I use the square one or the rectangular one?

Let's aim high now!

Fill in the missing **brackets**, **colons** and **ellipses** in these sentences.

1. I think I'll put my paintbrushes away or maybe I won't.
2. That painting is now what's the word I'm looking for?
3. You'll never believe where we went today to the art gallery!
4. Albert Namatjira born Elea Namatjira was a very successful artist.
5. I've drawn up a list of the items I need paints, brushes and an easel.
6. Albert Namatjira 1902–1959 painted landscapes of the Australian outback.
7. The artist finds inspiration everywhere at home, in the city and in the country.

Let's put it together now!

This student has left out some **conjunctions** and **punctuation marks** in this imaginary interview with the artist, Sidney Nolan. Use a red pen to make the corrections. There are seven mistakes altogether.

Sidney Nolan 1917–1992 is an important Australian artist. This is my imaginary interview with him.

Kathy: Good morning, Sidney.

Sidney Good morning.

Kathy: I'd like to start by asking you about your Ned Kelly paintings.

Sidney: looks amused Yes, I thought you might.

Kathy: They're still very popular. Why do you think that is?

Sidney: Mmm that's a difficult question to answer. I think it's I've used strong, simple lines. They look a bit like children's art. People seem to like that.

Kathy: Did you enjoy painting them?

Sidney: Well yes and no. They are popular today, I wasn't sure at the time that people would like them.

Let's have fun!

Aboriginal artworks often tell a story. The artists use symbols to represent people and things in nature. See if you can guess what the symbols in these sentences stand for.

1. When the rain stopped, we saw a beautiful 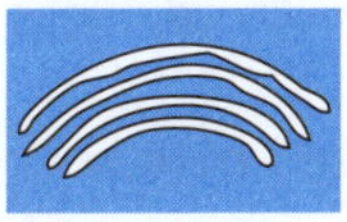 in the sky.
2. Before the clouds arrived, the 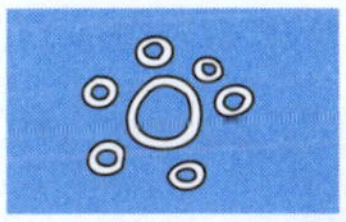 was shining brightly.
3. We couldn't cross the river because the 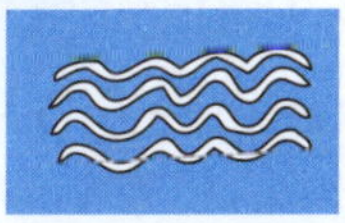 was flowing too strongly.

Here are some more symbols that often appear in Aboriginal art. Tick those that look like **brackets**, put a circle around those that look like **colons**, and put boxes around those that look like **ellipses**.

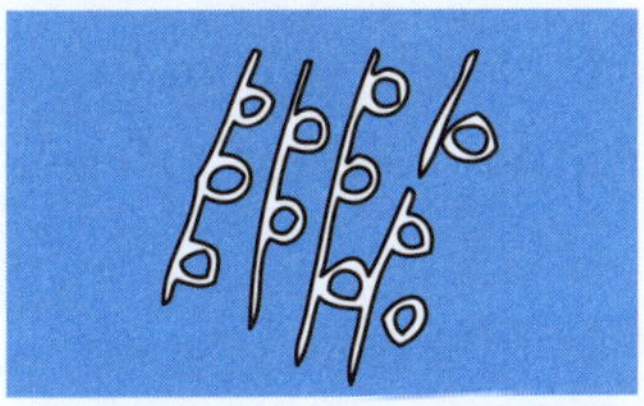

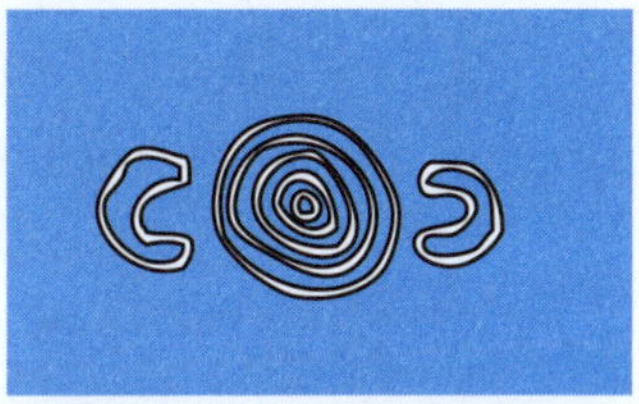

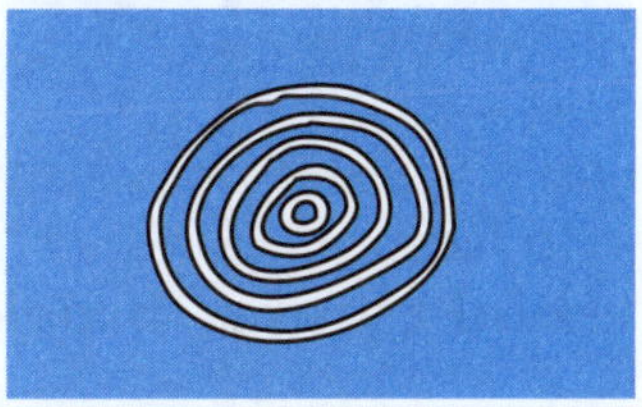

Let's have a test!

In questions 1–2, choose the word that completes the sentence correctly.

1. I have not been to the gallery ______________ the exhibition.

   ○ while ○ since ○ before ○ when

2. I like her paintings ______________ she uses bright colours.

   ○ because ○ unless ○ until ○ while

Which word does **not** complete the sentence correctly?

3. He painted the picture ______________ he went to the outback.

   ○ when ○ after ○ before ○ while

4. Which answer is similar in meaning to these two sentences?

   I bought the painting. I did not like it.

   ○ Although I liked the painting, I did not buy it.
   ○ While I like the painting, I did not buy it.
   ○ Although I did not like the painting, I bought it.
   ○ I will not buy the painting unless I like it.

5. Which is the best place for the ellipsis in this sentence?

   We ↑ walked into ↑ the gallery and ↑ there it ↑ was!

6. Which sentence has used brackets correctly?

   ○ (Artworld) the gallery's magazine, comes out once a month.
   ○ Artworld (the gallery's magazine) comes out once a month.
   ○ Artworld, the gallery's magazine, comes out (once) a month.
   ○ Artworld, the gallery's magazine, comes out once (a month).

In questions 7–8, show where the colons should go.

7. These are ↑ the things ↑ I like ↑ to paint ↑ mountains, trees and rivers.

8. I have an announcement ↑ to ↑ make ↑ the painting ↑ sold for $10 million!

Let's write now!

Find information on a well-known Australian artist, such as Arthur Boyd, Frederick McCubbin or Rosella Namok. Conduct an imaginary **interview** with the artist you have chosen. Use **adverbial clauses**, **brackets**, **colons** and **ellipses** in your interview.

Unit 14 Recycling

Focus
Modality; adverbs; abbreviations

Why recycling is important

Australia is the second biggest producer of rubbish in the world, which is certainly not something to be proud of. To control the amount of rubbish we produce, **we must recycle whatever we can**.

We should all think very carefully before we throw stuff in our rubbish bins, as it will probably end up in landfills. Not only are these taking up more and more space, but it also costs a lot of money to maintain them. Next time you put something in the bin, ask yourself if it can be recycled or reused in some way.

By recycling our rubbish, we could also be saving the earth. Paper, for example, comes from trees, so if we recycle it, **we might not have to chop down so many trees**. That is surely an argument in favour of recycling!

If we want to save the environment, recycling is definitely the way to go!

by Caleb

This is an **exposition**. Remember: an exposition expresses and gives reasons for an opinion, usually in order to convince others. Caleb uses **modal verbs** and **adverbs** to show how certain he is of the need to recycle.

Modal verbs are auxiliary verbs that show how certain we are about something. This is called **modality**.

Auxiliary verbs that show certainty have **high modality**; for example, **we must recycle whatever we can**.

Auxiliary verbs that show uncertainty have **low modality**; for example, **we might not have to chop down so many trees**.

Adverbs can also have modality.

Adverbs with high modality include *definitely*, *certainly*, *surely*, *always*, *never*.

Adverbs with low modality include *perhaps*, *maybe*, *usually*, *probably*, *sometimes*.

Let's find them!

Write down whether these auxiliary verbs and adverbs from the text show **high** or **low modality**.

1. certainly ______________________________
2. must ______________________________

3. probably ______________________________

4. could ______________________________

5. might not ______________________________

6. surely ______________________________

7. definitely ______________________________

Let's go to the next step!

Underline the **modal verbs** and **adverbs** in these sentences.

1. I always put my rubbish in the right bin.
2. We may produce less rubbish in the future.
3. One day they might be able to recycle plastic bags.
4. You must not put your old clothes in the recycling bin.
5. He never puts his scraps of paper in the recycling bin.
6. Recycling is something we should all be taking seriously.
7. Perhaps more people will start recycling and reusing things.

Tip!
Read through all of the questions before deciding which words to choose!

Let's aim high now!

Complete these sentences with a **modal verb** or **adverb** from the box. The instruction in brackets will help you choose the correct word. Use each word once.

definitely	never	might	must	always	perhaps	should

1. ______________ he'll recycle those bottles. (shows uncertainty)
2. We ______________ all be trying to produce less rubbish. (shows uncertainty)
3. I ______________ donate my old toys to the local church. (shows uncertainty)
4. She ______________ puts her empty bottles in the recycling bin. (shows certainty)
5. I will ______________ be taking these old clothes to the charity shop. (shows certainty)
6. My mother ______________ puts the vegetable peels on the compost heap. (shows certainty)
7. We ______________ start looking after the environment, before it is too late. (shows certainty)

A visit from KAB

Last week some people from **KAB** (**Keep Australia Beautiful**) came to our school to help us reduce the amount of rubbish we send to landfills. They told us that if all the rubbish in Australia was spread out, it would cover the state of Victoria!

They placed the garbage bins on the field next to Wattle Ave. Our teacher, Mr Barton, put us into groups and then we began the grubby task of sorting the rubbish into different categories. All the stuff from the garden and any bits of food went into a bin to be turned into compost. We put all other recyclable waste, e.g. plastic bottles, aluminium cans and paper products, into a different set of bins. Finally, we were left with a small pile of general rubbish for the landfill. Afterwards our principal, Dr Pearson, said that our school would be taking part in a recycling program with some other schools in New South Wales.

by Silvana

This is a **recount**. Remember: a recount tells about things that have already happened. Silvana uses **abbreviations**—shortened forms of words or phrases—while telling about the visit from KAB.

Abbreviations are the shortened forms of words or phrases; for example, **KAB** is the shortened form of **Keep Australia Beautiful**.

Let's find them!

Tip! The **abbreviations** of proper nouns start with capital letters.

Find these **abbreviations** and words in the text.

1. the abbreviation of *Avenue* ______________
2. the abbreviation of *Mister* ______________
3. the abbreviation of *for example* ______________
4. the abbreviation of *Doctor* ______________
5. the word that could be shortened to *Aus* ______________
6. the word that could be shortened to *Vic* ______________
7. the phrase that could be shortened to *NSW* ______________

Let's go to the next step!

In these sentences, one of the words in brackets is the correct **abbreviation** for the underlined word or phrase. Cross out the abbreviation that is wrong.
For example: When we lived in Queensland (~~Qsd~~, Qld), we were close to a tip.

1. Our nearest tip is six kilometres (klm/km) away.
2. The tip is at the end of Juniper Road (Rd/R).
3. I saw a documentary about recycling on Television (tele/TV).
4. There is even litter on the slopes of Mount (Mnt/Mt) Everest!
5. We are going to visit a recycling plant in August (Aug/Au).
6. There isn't a square metre (m/met) of their yard that isn't filled with rubbish.
7. The letter about the new recycling program went to our post office (Pof/PO) box.

Let's aim high now!

Use a dictionary to help you find what the **abbreviations** in these sentences stand for. The abbreviations are in bold.

1. The new landfill will be to the **NE** of the city. ____________________
2. The lady who works for KAB lives in Stanley **Cres.** ____________________
3. People from the **Dept** of Health told them to remove the rubbish. ____________________
4. My sister, who is at **uni**, told me how plastic bottles are recycled. ____________________
5. The **UN** is doing what it can to make people aware of the need to recycle. ____________________
6. **Prof** Julian Smith is coming to our school to tell us why recycling is important. ____________________
7. Our local **MP** wants supermarkets to stop providing customers with plastic bags. ____________________

Let's put it together now!

This student has written three **abbreviations** incorrectly and has left out these **modal verbs** and **adverbs** in this part of his exposition.

Use the words from the box to complete the text and use a red pen to make the corrections.

could	must	never	definitely

We ________________ all try to reuse or recycle things as much as possible. If you have old towels or blankets, the rspca will ________________ take them. You ________________ also take your old ink cartridges to the shop next to st Mark's College. And ________________ throw away clothes and toys that are still in good condition. Let someone else enjoy them. To find a charity near you that you can donate them to, go to WWW.auscharity.org.

Let's have fun!

Tip!
You must use all of the letters!

1. Recycle the letters in the rubbish bin by turning them into **modal verbs** and **adverbs** and placing them on the cans. Use the letters and number of blocks on each can as clues.

2. Place an **abbreviation** from the box on each of these packages. The description on the package will help you choose the right abbreviation.

US	Mrs	NZ	NT	UK	Dr	VIP	Capt.

Let's have a test!

1 Which word in this sentence is a modal verb?

I will recycle whatever I can, as I definitely want to help save the planet.

◯ will ◯ can ◯ definitely ◯ want

2 Which pair of words completes this sentence correctly?

You __________ sort through that rubbish as it __________ contain bacteria.

◯ must, can't ◯ can, will
◯ can't, might ◯ should, mustn't

3 Which word in this sentence is a modal adverb?

We could probably produce less rubbish if we tried a bit harder.

◯ could ◯ probably
◯ less ◯ tried

4 Which word does **not** complete this sentence correctly?

My mum has __________ tried to recycle and reuse in the past.

◯ always ◯ definitely ◯ must ◯ certainly

In questions 5–8, show which option is the correct abbreviation of the underlined word.

5 The rubbish in the bag weighs 10 kilograms.

◯ kg ◯ kgs
◯ kilo ◯ kilogs

6 The post script at the end of her e-mail contained more information about recycling.

◯ POST ◯ PST
◯ PS ◯ PSST

7 I sprinkled a teaspoon of disinfectant over the pile of rubbish.

◯ tsp ◯ teasp
◯ ts ◯ tspn

8 They collected our rubbish at six this morning.

◯ pm ◯ am
◯ ad ◯ bc

Let's write now!

Find information on recycling in books or on the Internet, and then write an **exposition** in which you put forward reasons for recycling plastic bags, cardboard boxes or any other item. Use **modal verbs** and **adverbs** to persuade readers to your point of view, and try to use one or two **abbreviations.**

Unit 15 Best sellers

Focus
Apostrophes that show contraction; apostrophes that show ownership

Bridge to Terabithia

Bridge to Terabithia, by Katherine Paterson, is set in a country area in the deep south of America in the mid-20th century. **It's** a story of friendship, imagination and dealing with loss. The main characters in the book are ten-year-old Jesse Aarons and Leslie Burke. He's unsure of himself; she's full of confidence. He'd been the fastest runner in the fifth grade—until Leslie arrived. But this doesn't stop them from becoming firm friends. As Leslie notes, "... we might as well be friends. There's no one else close by".

One day Jess and Leslie discover an old tree fort in the woods, and that's what gives Leslie the idea for their secret, magic kingdom—Terabithia. Leslie encourages Jess to accept himself as he is and not to pay too much attention to what others think about him. Jess has never been happier. But then tragedy strikes, and Jess's world is turned upside down.

This is the best book I've read this year. I believe we can all learn something from it. It taught me about the value of true friendship and the happiness we get from using our imaginations and being ourselves. I can thoroughly recommend it.

by Carrie

This is a **review**. A review tells and gives opinions about books, films and shows. Carrie uses **apostrophes** in place of the missing letters to shorten words in her review of the novel *Bridge to Terabithia*.

Contractions

- are formed when two words are joined to make one, shorter word; for example, **It's** is short for **It is**.
- have **apostrophes (')** in place of the missing letters; for example, in *It's*, the apostrophe takes the place of the *i* in *is*.

Rule!

Watch out for these tricky words:

- It's hard to say '**willn't**' for **will not**, so we say **won't**.
- We use **its** without the apostrophe when it's a possessive pronoun; for example, **The book has lost <u>its</u> cover.**
- The word **who's** is short for **who is**, while **whose** means '**who it belongs to**'; for example, **the man <u>who's</u> an author/the man <u>whose</u> book it is.**

Let's find them!

Find these **contractions** in the text.

1. he is ________________
2. she is ________________
3. he had ________________
4. does not ________________
5. there is ________________
6. that is ________________
7. I have ________________

Let's go to the next step!

Use a red pen to fill in the missing **apostrophes** in the **contractions** in these sentences.

1. This term were reading a book thats on the best seller list.
2. Theyre discussing the book that theyve just finished reading.
3. Ill give the book to my friend to read when Ive finished with it.
4. I wouldve finished the book sooner if Id had more time to read it.
5. I couldnt find the book in the library so I havent finished my project.
6. I dont want to read that book because my friend says it isnt interesting.
7. He wont read this book because someone told him its got scary parts in it.

Let's aim high now!

Tip!
Be careful! Some sentences have two sets of words that can be written as **contractions**.

Underline the words that can be joined to make one word and then write the **contractions** in the spaces.

For example:

I may have read that book already. may've

1. Who is going to be the first one to read this book? ________________
2. You should not force people to read books they do not like. ________________
   ____
3. They will hear the authors speak about their books at the book fair. ________________
4. You must not read that book as it is not suitable for young children.
   ____
5. This author is an amazing writer and I intend reading all of his books. ________________
6. I have not read any of this author's books, but I believe they are very good. ________________
7. They said they would try to find the book, but they were not sure if it was still in print.
   ____

Boy Overboard

Morris Gleitzman's novel, *Boy Overboard*, highlights the effects of war on people's lives. The book's narrator, Jamal, is an eleven-year-old Afghani boy who is passionate about soccer. Unfortunately, soccer has been banned by Afghanistan's Taliban government. But that's not why Jamal's family is forced to flee the country. The government has found out about his mum's illegal school for girls, and her life is in danger.

Jamal, his parents and his feisty little sister, Bibi, make their way to Pakistan, and from there they board a battered boat headed for Australia, where they hope to start a new life. But their problems are far from over ...

This is a great book. It's sad, funny and exciting at the same time. **The main characters' temperaments** are all different, but they're all believable. Bibi is just like my little sister! Some things made me angry, like the soldiers' cruelty and the smugglers' greed, but other things reminded me a lot of my family, like the parents' concern for **their children's safety**. We aren't told whether Jamal's family made it to Australia, but I hope they did.

by Jonathan

This is another **review**. Jonathan uses **apostrophes** to show ownership in his review of the novel *Boy Overboard*.

Apostrophes are also used to show **ownership**; for example, **Morris Gleitzman's novel**. The apostrophe shows that the novel **belongs to** (or was written by) Morris Gleitzman.

Rule!

- If there is one owner, the apostrophe comes before the *s*; for example, **Gleitzman's novel**.
- If there is more than one owner, the apostrophe comes after the *s*; for example, **The main characters' temperaments**.
- For irregular plurals, such as **men**, **children** and **sheep**, the apostrophe always comes before the *s*; for example, **their children's safety**.

Let's find them!

Who or what do these people or things **belong to** in the text?

1. lives ______
2. the Taliban government ______
3. the family ______
4. the illegal school ______
5. cruelty ______
6. greed ______
7. concern ______

Tip!

Normal plurals do not have apostrophes because they don't own anything; for example, **There are lots of characters in this book.**

Let's go to the next step!

Use a red pen to fill in the missing **apostrophes** in these sentences.

1. Those bookcases shelves need to be fixed.
2. I like the look of this books cover, so I might read it.
3. This is the tenth week that the authors new book has been on the best seller list.
4. I found this book in the childrens section, but I think it belongs with the adults books.
5. This storys ending is very sad, unlike the other stories endings, which are much happier.
6. They announced the book of the year after counting both the critics votes and the peoples votes.
7. Some students in our class are going to the writers festival, which is being held in the citys largest conference centre.

Let's aim high now!

Rewrite the underlined phrases in these sentences with an **apostrophe**.
For example: The name of the author appears on the front page. The author's name

1. I can't find the name of the illustrator on this book.

   ____

2. I have quoted the words of the writer in my review.

   ____

3. The plot of the novel moves at a fast, exciting pace.

   ____

4. The shelves of the bookshop are full of best sellers!

   ____

5. The works of certain authors are well known throughout the world.

   ____

6. In his new book, the backgrounds of the characters are all different.

   ____

7. The books of JRR Tolkien have sold millions of copies through the years.

   ____

Let's put it together now!

This student has left out some **apostrophes** and put others where they don't belong in this part of his review. Use a red pen to make the corrections. There are seven mistakes altogether.

One of my favourite books' is Gillian Rubinsteins science fiction novel *Space Demons*. Its about a group of children who get sucked into a computer game and have to fight their way out of it. The characters true personalities are revealed by the way they act once theyre inside the game. The more hateful their thoughts, the harder it is to break the games hold on them.

Im not a great fan of computer games, but I really enjoyed this book, and I think you will too.

Let's have fun!

Fit the words in the book into the spaces. The number of circles and the position of the **apostrophes** are your clues.

1. ○○○○○'○
2. ○○○'○○
3. ○'○
4. ○○○○○○'○
5. ○○'○
6. ○○○○○○'
7. ○○○○'○○
8. ○○○'○
9. ○○○○'○
10. ○○○○○○○○'○

Let's have a test!

1 Which sentence has been punctuated correctly?

- ◯ Max do'esn't know what the book is about.
- ◯ Max doe'snt know what the book is about.
- ◯ Max does'nt know what the book is about.
- ◯ Max doesn't know what the book is about.

In questions 2–3, which pair of words completes the sentence correctly?

2 If ____________ going to read the book, ____________ have to get it from the library.

◯ your, you'll ◯ you're, you'll ◯ their, they'll ◯ his, he'll

3 ____________ an interesting book, but I don't like ____________ cover.

◯ Its, it's ◯ It's, it's ◯ Its, its ◯ It's, its

4 Which underlined words could be replaced with *We're*?

- ◯ We were going to read that book.
- ◯ We are going to read that book.
- ◯ Were we going to read that book?
- ◯ Where are we going to read that book?

5 Which words complete the sentence correctly?

This ____________ have been removed.

◯ books page's ◯ books' pages
◯ book's pages ◯ books pages'

6 In questions 6–7, choose the word that completes the sentence correctly.

Those ____________ books are best sellers.

◯ peoples' ◯ person's
◯ people's ◯ peoples

7 This book is about a ____________ fight to save the gorillas.

◯ woman's ◯ women's ◯ womans' ◯ womens'

8 Which pair of words completes the sentence correctly?

Which ____________ have made this ____________ best seller list?

◯ books', years' ◯ book's, years' ◯ books, year's ◯ books', years

Let's write now!

Choose a book that you have enjoyed reading and write a **review** of it. Use **apostrophes** to show where letters have been left out in **contractions** and to show ownership.

Unit 16 Where does it come from?

Focus
Direct speech; speech marks; indirect speech

The Apple Tree

Mandy was reading a Harry Potter book when her three-year-old brother Tom came bursting into the room.

"Mandy, Mandy, look what I've got!" he shouted excitedly.

"It's an apple," she said, and carried on reading.

"Mandy, Mandy," Tom continued, "do you know where it comes from?"

"From the fridge," said Mandy, without looking up.

"But where did it come from before that, Mandy?" asked Tom.

"An apple tree," said Mandy. "Now leave me alone, I'm trying to read."

"Where did the apple tree come from, Mandy?" persisted Tom.

Mandy sighed. She adored her little brother, and she always tried to answer his endless questions, no matter how bizarre or annoying they were. "It comes from a seed," she said, more kindly this time.

"But where does the seed come from, Mandy?"

"From an apple," said Mandy, turning her attention back to her book.

Tom looked puzzled for a moment, but then his face lit up and he ran out of the room.

This is part of a **narrative**. Remember: a narrative tells a story. The author uses **direct speech** with **speech marks** to show the exact words that Tom and Mandy said in their conversation about where an apple comes from.

Direct speech

- quotes the exact words that someone says in a text; for example, **"Mandy, Mandy, look what I've got!"** are Tom's exact words.
- always has **speech** or **quotation marks** around the spoken words; for example, **"Mandy, Mandy, look what I've got!" he shouted excitedly**.

Rule! When someone starts speaking for the first time, the first word they say always starts with a capital letter, even if it comes after a comma; for example, **He shouted, "Look what I've got!"**

Tip! The comma, full stop, question mark or exclamation mark that comes at the end of what someone says goes inside the speech mark; for example, **"Mandy, Mandy, look what I've got!" he shouted excitedly.**

Let's find them!

Find these sentences in the text and fill in the missing **punctuation marks**.

1. It's an apple she said, and carried on reading.
2. Mandy, Mandy Tom continued, do you know where it comes from
3. But where did it come from before that, Mandy Tom asked.
4. Now leave me alone, I'm trying to read
5. Where did the apple tree come from, Mandy persisted Tom.
6. It comes from a seed she said, more kindly this time.
7. But where does the seed come from, Mandy

Let's go to the next step!

Underline the **exact words** that each person says in these sentences, including the **punctuation**.

For example: "Did you know that wool comes from a sheep?" asked William.

1. Mum said, "I didn't know that cork comes from oak trees."
2. "I thought these oranges were from Queensland," said Joel.
3. "Look at this beautiful outfit," said Aunt Sarah. "I got it in Paris!"
4. "Most of the films in our cinemas come from America," said Chrissy.
5. "I've found out where this necklace comes from!" exclaimed Ramina.
6. "Grandma says these silver candlesticks come from Russia," said Ursula.
7. "Mum says I get my good looks from her and my brains from Dad!" announced Cindy.

Let's aim high now!

Use a red pen to fill in the missing **speech marks** in these sentences.

1. Where did all this water come from? asked Mum.
2. Which animal do these horns come from? asked Lara.
3. Thousands of items are made from oil, explained our science teacher.
4. These tusks, said the lady at the museum, are from a woolly mammoth.
5. Today we learnt that butter and cheese come from milk, said the little boy.
6. May I hand out the souvenirs I got for everyone while I was in Japan? asked Zac.
7. Divers have found a shipwreck dating from the 1st century, announced the newsreader.

The Apple Tree

When Mum went outside to hang out the washing, Tom was playing in his sandbox. **Mum asked him what he was doing.** He said he was digging a hole. Then Mum saw him put his apple in the hole and cover it with sand. She asked him why he was burying his apple. Tom said he was growing an apple tree. He said Mandy had told him that apple trees come from seeds, and that the seeds are in the apple. He announced proudly that he'd worked it all out. If the seeds are in the apple, then the tree that produces the apple must come from the apple! Mum said that it wasn't that simple. But Tom would have none of it. He said that if Mandy said that was what happened, it must be true!

This is another part of the **narrative**. The author uses **indirect speech** without **speech marks** to show what Mum and Tom said about growing an apple tree.

Indirect or **reported speech**

- tells what someone said without using their exact words; for example, **Mum asked him what he was doing.** (These are not Mum's exact words.)
- does not have **speech marks**.

Let's find them!

Underline the sentence in the text that is similar in meaning to each of these sentences.

1. "What are you doing?" asked Mum.
2. "I'm digging a hole," he said.
3. "Why are you burying your apple?" she asked.
4. "I'm growing an apple tree," said Tom.
5. "I've worked it all out," he announced proudly.
6. "It's not that simple," said Mum.
7. "If Mandy says that's what happens, it must be true," he said.

Tip!

Remember: when you write **direct speech** as **indirect speech**, you have to change the verbs from the present tense to the past tense.

Let's go to the next step!

Complete each sentence with the correct **verb** in brackets (the past tense verb). Cross out the one that is wrong.

For example: He said that he (~~is~~, was) from England.

1. I asked them where they (have, had) found the ring.
2. He said they (were, are) looking for the source of the river.
3. The librarian said that she (will, would) help us find the information.
4. She asked us if we (know, knew) which story the character was from.
5. She said that she (doesn't, didn't) know where the money (has, had) come from.
6. The girl explained that she (was, is) trying to find out where the carving came from.
7. Dad said that we (shall, should) ask the neighbours where they (have, had) found the shells.

Let's aim high now!

Complete the second sentence in each pair by filling in the missing words. Remember to change the tense of the **verb** and, where necessary, the **pronoun**.

For example: "I don't know where the dust comes from," she said.
She said that <u>she didn't know</u> where the dust came from.

1. "The milk is from the farm," he said.

   He said that ______________________ from the farm.

2. "I know where to find the picture," said Mr Norton.

   Mr Norton said that ______________________ where to find the picture.

3. "The noise is coming from the roof," said the man.

   The man said that ____________________________________ from the roof.

4. "I have no idea which book the recipe is from," said the lady.

   The lady said that ____________ no idea which book the recipe __________ from.

5. "The dance troupe comes from Russia," said Mrs Caro.

   Mrs Caro said that ______________________________________ from Russia.

6. "I will try to find out where the rabbit's burrow is," said the man.

   The man said that _______________ to find out where the rabbit's burrow ______.

7. "Cold weather is coming from the south," warned the lady from the weather bureau.

   The lady from the weather bureau warned that _________________ from the south.

Let's put it together now!

This student has made the following mistakes in this part of her narrative: she has written the underlined words in the wrong tense and has put five lots of **speech marks** in the wrong place. Use a red pen to make the corrections for her.

"I bet you don't know where milk comes from", said Milly.

"Yes I do"! replied Sam indignantly, "It comes from the supermarket"!

"No it doesn't", said Milly, "it comes from a cow."

"Oh that's really silly, Milly," said Sam. "I've never seen a cow in the supermarket before".

Milly <u>tells</u> ____________ Sam that he didn't know anything, but Sam said he obviously <u>knows</u> ____________ more than Milly about where milk came from.

Let's have fun!

The words and punctuation in the answers to these questions are all muddled up. Sort them out and then write the answers correctly in the spaces. Answers may be in either **direct** or **indirect speech**.

1. Q: "Where does this structure come from?" asked the teacher.
   A: comes Suzy " from , It Ancient Egypt " . replied

2. Q: "Where does this person come from?"
   A: He Tom fairy " a tale , from . comes " well-known answered

3. Q: "Where does this animal come from?" Mum asked Tim.
   A: It " Taronga " said Zoo from Tim in Sydney , comes .

4. Q: "Where does this object come from?" asked the lady.
   A: the from Joanne . came said queen's it that crown

5. Q: "Where does this loaf come from?" asked Dad.
   A: came said down the road Mum . from the bakery that it

Let's have a test!

1 Which sentence has the correct punctuation?

- ◯ "The cyclist came from nowhere", said the driver.
- ◯ "the cyclist came from nowhere," said the driver.
- ◯ "The cyclist came from nowhere, said the driver."
- ◯ "The cyclist came from nowhere," said the driver.

2 Where do the missing commas go in this sentence?

"I don't know where Grandma ◯ got this locket ◯ " ◯ said Mum ◯ "or these rings."

In questions 3–4, which punctuation mark is missing?

3 "Do you know where this card came from" asked Lilly.

◯ . ◯ , ◯ ? ◯ !

4 "I've finally found out where the bees are coming from" exclaimed Dad.

◯ ? ◯ ! ◯ . ◯ ,

5 Which sentence has the correct punctuation?

- ◯ My friend asked me if I knew where the new boy came from.
- ◯ My friend asked me if I knew where the new boy came from?
- ◯ My friend asked me "If I knew where the new boy came from?"
- ◯ My friend asked me "if I knew where the new boy came from."

6 Which word can be left out of this sentence without changing its meaning?

My teacher said that she knew where my book was.

◯ My ◯ that ◯ she ◯ where

7 Which pair of words completes the sentence correctly?

Mark said he ______________ know where the balloons ______________ come from.

- ◯ didn't, has
- ◯ don't, had
- ◯ didn't, had
- ◯ doesn't, had

8 Which option does **not** complete the sentence correctly?

Lisa said she ______________ asked them where they came from.

- ◯ should have
- ◯ should've
- ◯ shouldn't have
- ◯ shouldn't

Let's write now!

What happened after Tom planted the apple? Continue the **narrative**, using some **direct** and **indirect speech** in the remaining paragraphs.

Unit 17 Colours

Focus
Rhyme and figures of speech: similes and metaphors; onomatopoeia and alliteration

Colour poems

Green is ... as cool as the forest on a hot summer's day
as graceful as the trees when they start to sway
as fresh as the grass that has just been **mown**
as bright as the leaves that are newly **grown**.

White is ... like the sunlight that hurts my eyes
like the ash when the fire dies
like the snow—crisp and cold
like our hair when we grow old.

Blue things ...
The sky is the canopy over my head
The lake is the mirror that reflects my smiles
This book is a memory of words that I've read
My blue teddy bear helps me cope with life's trials.

by Year 5 students

These are **poems**. Poems use words in imaginative ways to express ideas or to describe people or things. The Year 5 students use **similes** and **metaphors** to compare things and **rhyme** to give their poems structure while imaginatively describing what the colours green, white and blue mean to them.

Figures of speech use words to create visual images and sound effects.

Similes are figures of speech that compare objects or ideas using the words *like* or *as*.

For example: **Green is ... as cool as the forest on a hot summer's day. White is ... like the sunlight that hurts my eyes**.

Metaphors are figures of speech that make comparisons where one thing is said to be something else.

For example: **The sky is the canopy over my head**.

Rhyme in poetry is a pattern of words that have similar sounds, usually at the ends of lines; for example, **mown** and **grown**. Rhyme adds structure and rhythm to a poem.

Let's find them!

Find three **similes**, two **metaphors** and two pairs of **rhyming words** in the text. Don't use the words in bold.

______ ______

______ ______

______ ______

______

Let's go to the next step!

Write down whether these sentences contain **similes**, **metaphors** or **rhyming words**.

For example: A layer of snow covered the fields like a white blanket. simile

1. She has a heart of gold. ______
2. His hair is as black as coal. ______
3. The road was a ribbon of silver moonlight. ______
4. The cat's eyes are as green as emeralds. ______
5. Silver droplets on the glass, waiting for the storm to pass. ______
6. We came upon a little town, its roads were narrow, rough and brown. ______

Let's aim high now!

Complete these **similes**, **metaphors** and **rhymes** with a word from the box.

shampoo	green	orange	sight	gold	red	white

1. The bride's dress looked like a ______ meringue!
2. The sun was a shimmering ______ ball on the horizon.
3. We were given the ______ light to go ahead with the project.
4. The little boy was as good as ______ while his mother was away.
5. We expected them to roll out the ______ carpet for us when we got there.
6. Out of the blackness of the night emerged a terrifying ______!
7. My sister smells of soap and ______,
to me she smells like the colour blue.

The sounds I heard today

Today I heard these sounds …

The beep-beep-beeping of my blue alarm clock

My mother's screams when she smelled my brown sock

The water swishing in the kitchen sink

My little sister's squeals when Mum dressed her in pink

A screeching siren as a red fire engine flew by

The crunch as I bit into a golden pie

The raucous squawks of a big black crow

The rustling of leaves when the wind started to blow.

Those were the sounds I heard today.

by Henry

This is another **poem**. Henry uses **onomatopoeia** to imitate the sounds he heard and **alliteration** to add rhythm and energy to his poem.

Onomatopoeia is language that imitates sounds; for example, **screams**. It adds energy and interest to poems and narratives.

Alliteration is the repetition of consonants in a sequence of words; for example, **My mother's screams when she smelled my brown sock**. Alliteration adds rhythm, energy and interest to poems and other literary texts.

Let's find them!

Find four examples of **onomatopoeia** and three examples of **alliteration** in the text and write them in the spaces below. Don't use the words in bold.

Tip!

Alliteration makes language easier to remember. That's why there's so much of it in nursery rhymes and advertisements!

Let's go to the next step!

Underline the **onomatopoeia** and circle the **alliteration** in these sentences. Some sentences contain both figures of speech.
For example: A big black bug was buzzing around the room.

1. Fierce orange flames flew into the air.
2. The tin of yellow paint clattered to the floor.
3. I heard a crash and then everything went black.
4. The cute cat purred softly as I tickled its tummy.
5. A flock of colourful birds was chattering in the tree.
6. Our neighbour has just bought a sleek silver sports car.
7. A gruesome, grey, ghostly figure jumped out from behind the door.

Let's aim high now!

The sentences in Column A contain examples of **alliteration** and those in Column B contain examples of **onomatopoeia**. Shade the matching pairs the same colour. The first one has been done for you.

Column A	Column B
1 Six red roosters rushed across the yard.	They growled menacingly.
2 The pink pig foraged for food.	It chuckled gleefully.
3 The silver snake slithered closer.	It grunted contentedly.
4 The dangerous brown dogs dashed towards us.	It squawked noisily at a passing crow.
5 The great grey elephant lumbered across the road.	It reared its head and hissed.
6 The pretty purple parrot was perched on a pole.	They all crowed at the same time.
7 The keen-eyed kookaburra spotted a green grasshopper.	It stopped, threw back its ears and trumpeted loudly.

Let's put it together now!

This student is unsure about which words to choose to complete his poem. Help him choose words from the box that fit in with the **rhyme** scheme of the poem and that complete an example of a **metaphor**, **simile**, **alliteration** and **onomatopoeia**.

The colours of nature

Nature ______ a jigsaw of different hues
Of the deepest greens and the softest ______
Nature's ______ a tapestry, woven with threads
Of beautiful browns and bright bold ______
The colours of Nature stand happily together
Lavender next to grey; purple next to ______
They ______ us when thunder ______ overhead
They soothe us in the evening when the sun goes to bed.

reds	was
pinks	blacks
amuse	blues
threaten	silver
as	gold
like	whispers
is	roars

Let's have fun!

Complete this crossword puzzle with the names of colours. The clues will help you find the right ones. Notice that some of the clues contain **similes**, **metaphors** and **alliteration**.

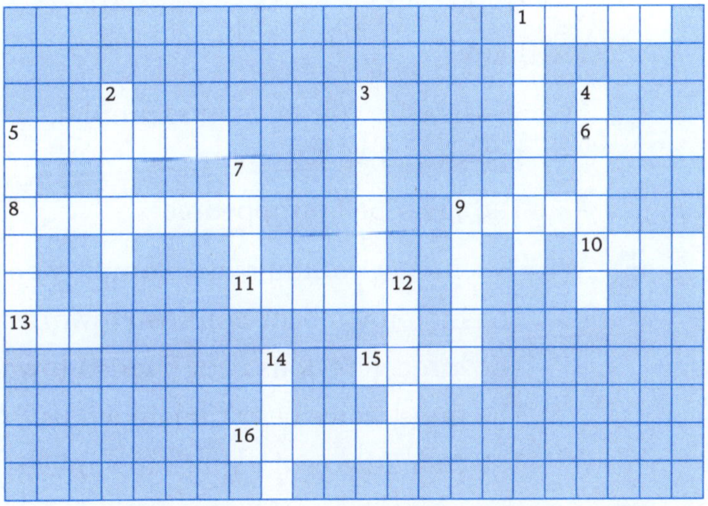

Across:

1. He's the ______ of the crop!
5. a bright red colour
6. "My love is like a red, red ______" is a line from a well-known poem.
8. This colour is also the name of a purple flower.
9. as ______ as a berry
10. All that glitters is not ______.
11. To have a ______ belly is to be a coward.
13. as ______ as a cherry
15. If someone is very healthy, they are said to be in the ______.
16. He started playing very well; he had hit a ______ patch.

Down:

1. a very vivid red colour
2. as ______ as grass
3. one of the colours of the rainbow
4. You can't compare an apple and an ______.
5. Every cloud has a ______ lining.
7. Clever people are said to have lots of ______ matter.
9. He is the ______ sheep of the family.
12. as ______ as a sheet
14. It happens once in a ______ moon.

Let's have a test!

1. Which sentence contains a simile?
   - ◯ The Blue Mountains are not really blue.
   - ◯ From a distance, the Blue Mountains look like a dragon's back.
   - ◯ From a distance, the Blue Mountains look blue.
   - ◯ There are no dragons in the Blue Mountains.

2. Which words complete this sentence correctly?

   The boy's face ______________ red as a beetroot.
   - ◯ was like
   - ◯ is like
   - ◯ is as
   - ◯ as like

3. Which sentence contains a metaphor?
   - ◯ She has a heart of gold.
   - ◯ Her heart is like gold.
   - ◯ She is as good as gold.
   - ◯ She likes the colour gold.

4. Which word completes this metaphor correctly?

   A lion's teeth ______________ white daggers.
   - ◯ is
   - ◯ as
   - ◯ like
   - ◯ are

5. Which word best completes these lines?

   He wandered down the wide brown road

   On his back a heavy ______________.
   - ◯ cargo
   - ◯ parcel
   - ◯ load
   - ◯ package

6. Which sentence contains an example of onomatopoeia?
   - ◯ The silver bell fell.
   - ◯ The silver bell tinkled.
   - ◯ The silver bell disappeared.
   - ◯ The silver bell broke.

7. Which sentence contains an example of alliteration?
   - ◯ The big brown bear bounded towards us.
   - ◯ The large, ferocious bear headed towards us.
   - ◯ The huge, fierce bear threatened us.
   - ◯ The cute little bear walked towards us.

8. Which word best completes this sentence?

   The ______________ wind whistled around the old grey house.
   - ◯ serious
   - ◯ sweet
   - ◯ dark
   - ◯ wild

Let's write now!

Write a **poem** about your favourite colour. Try to make some of the lines **rhyme**, and use some of the **figures of speech** that you have learnt about in this unit.

Unit 18 Like and unlike

Focus
Antonyms; synonyms; nominalisation

This is an **advertisement**. An advertisement persuades people to buy or do things. The advertiser uses **antonyms** to compare and contrast different types of shoes and their effects on children's feet, and **synonyms** to add variety to the text.

These are **sad** feet. These are **happy** feet.

Research has shown that badly shaped, rigid shoes are harmful to young feet.

Happyfeet shoes **allow** children's feet to behave like feet!

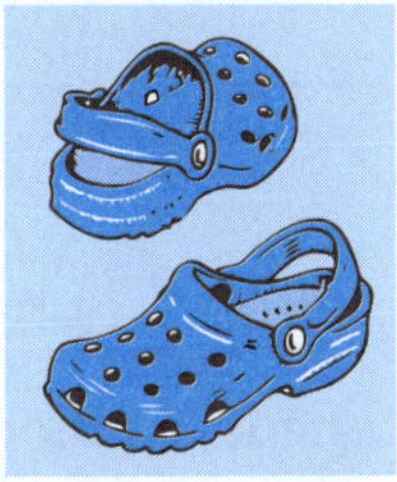

☑ They have broad toe boxes.

☑ They are made from soft, flexible materials that **let** feet breathe.

Happyfeet shoes tick a lot of other boxes as well.

☑ They are manufactured from recycled materials.

☑ They are excellent value for money.

☑ They come in a wide range of bright colours and designs.

Next time you buy shoes for your child, choose Happyfeet!

Available at all leading department stores and online.

Antonyms
- are words with opposite meanings; for example, **sad** and **happy**.
- compare and contrast people, animals, places, objects, situations and events.

Synonyms
- are words with similar meanings; for example, **allow** and **let**.
- add variety and interest to texts.

Let's find them!

Find these **antonyms** and **synonyms** in the text. Write the antonym of

1. tired ______________________
2. rough ______________________
3. sore ______________________
4. rigid ______________________

Write the synonym of

5. good ______________________________

6. broad ______________________________

7. made ______________________________

Let's go to the next step!

Complete each sentence with the correct **antonym** from the box.

repulsive	seldom	crooked	compulsory	build	dull	scarce

1. In some countries food is abundant, while in others it is ______________.
2. Playing chess at school is voluntary, but playing sport is ______________.
3. It rains frequently in equatorial rainforests, but very ______________ in deserts.
4. The lines in my book are straight, but in my friend's book they're ______________.
5. I find many animals attractive to look at, but there are some that are ______________.
6. Most children would rather listen to interesting stories than to ______________ ones.
7. They are going to demolish that old tower and ______________ a new one in its place.

Let's aim high now!

Choose a **synonym** from the box for each underlined word in these sentences. Write the synonym in the space at the end of the sentence.

For example: She walked quickly down the road. briskly

champion	feeble	choose	furious	stubborn
praised	genuine	disastrous	wealth	imitate
relevant	misplaced	abroad	harbour	

1. These shoes are made from real leather. ______________
2. The old lady is still very weak after her illness. ______________
3. When Mum saw the mess I had made, she was livid! ______________
4. They commended me for my performance in the school play. ______________
5. When I refused to budge, Mum accused me of being obstinate. ______________
6. We had a postcard from our neighbours, who are travelling overseas. ______________
7. My sister is upset because she has lost her favourite pair of earrings. ______________

Latest apps for children aged 9+

Galaxy Quest, the latest app from Space Age Studios, is guaranteed to provide children in the 9–12-year age group with hours of enjoyment. To score points, players have to pilot their spacecraft through the Milky Way Galaxy until they reach the **safety** of Earth 2 (a planet that's almost identical to Earth) in the Andromeda Galaxy. Along the way they pass through hostile environments that are as unlike Earth as you can get! Each environment has its own set of obstacles, which must be overcome to progress to the next level.

The images are bright and cheerful, and the variety of environments and challenges provides a high level of interest, excitement and entertainment. An added bonus is the factual information the game provides of planets like Mars and Jupiter, which should please parents who prefer their children to play games with an educational content.

At only $2.99, this app offers great value for money!

This is a **review**. Remember: a review tells and gives opinions about books, movies and other forms of entertainment. The reviewer uses **nominalised** words to name concepts and ideas while reviewing the app *Galaxy Quest*.

Verbs and adjectives can be turned into **nouns**, usually by adding suffixes. This is called **nominalisation**. Nominalisation is used to name concepts and ideas.

For example: the noun **safety** is formed from the adjective **safe**.

Let's find them!

Tip!

Nominalised words are abstract nouns. They make our speech and writing sound more formal.

Find these **nominalised** words in the text. Write the **noun** that is formed from

1. the verb *enjoy* ____________
2. the adjective *various* ____________
3. the adjective *interested* ____________
4. the verb *excite* ____________
5. the verb *entertain* ____________
6. the verb *inform* ____________
7. the adjective *valuable* ____________

Let's go to the next step!

Choose a suffix to add to each verb or adjective below to turn it into a **noun**. Write the new word in the correct column. The first one has been done for you.

Tip! Use a dictionary to check your spelling!

Verb/ adjective	dom	ness	ment	ion
busy		business		
wise				
enjoy				
explain				
happy				
bore				
attract				
announce				
create				
star				
punctuate				
pollute				
forgive				
like				

Let's aim high now!

Complete these sentences by turning the verbs or adjectives in brackets into **nouns**. For example: There is always (confuse) confusion over which twin is which.

1. The boys share an (enthusiastic) ____________ for basketball.
2. I love the (mild) ____________ of autumn and the (fresh) ____________ of spring.
3. The (warm) ____________ of the sand contrasted with the (ice) ____________ of the water.
4. We couldn't hide our (astonish) ____________ when our teacher came to school wearing odd shoes.
5. Some rulers are known for their (kind) ____________ and others for their (cruel) ____________.
6. The (different) ____________ between the sisters is that one has more (confident) ____________ than the other.
7. Everyone was impressed by her (willing) ____________ to help, and upset by his (unwilling) ____________ to lend a hand.

Let's put it together now!

The Year 5 teacher gave her students this advertisement and asked them to find the following:

- antonyms for the words *alike*, *mild* and *sweet*.
- synonyms for the words *delicious* and *polite*.
- two verbs that have had suffixes added to them to turn them into nouns.

She asked her students to underline the antonyms, circle the synonyms and put boxes around the nouns.

This student has chosen the wrong words. Help him find the right ones by underlining the **antonyms** in red, the **synonyms** in blue and the **nouns** in green.

Treat your taste buds to an explosion of different flavours at Cafe Marcel's.
Try our spicy curries, savoury crepes, scrumptious desserts and wide selection of pies and pastries.
Our friendly staff are waiting to serve you!

Let's have fun!

Tip!
The words go forwards, backwards, up and down.

Find these words in the wordsearch puzzle

- **antonyms** of straight, difficult, wild, shiny and fresh.
- **synonyms** of tall, lots, powerful, valuable and ancient.
- **nouns** that have been formed from the verbs free, revise and amuse.
- **nouns** that have been formed from the adjectives beautiful and ugly.

b	x	t	v	s	t	y	l	y	a	c	f	j	m	l
e	e	a	g	h	d	k	l	n	c	i	e	a	s	y
a	o	m	p	r	l	q	u	a	s	s	x	b	e	g
u	y	e	k	l	o	p	d	m	s	y	z	d	h	h
t	a	m	x	f	y	g	w	j	x	a	i	p	f	g
y	c	n	e	i	p	l	d	w	q	m	g	x	h	i
j	g	k	f	r	e	e	d	o	m	z	j	k	r	h
p	l	n	f	n	v	c	s	g	h	s	t	a	l	e
r	n	o	k	l	s	x	b	h	a	x	w	t	h	m
e	r	i	i	e	s	s	e	n	i	l	g	u	b	c
c	q	s	t	s	v	z	x	t	u	i	a	q	f	s
i	u	i	u	r	h	s	j	v	g	n	o	r	t	s
o	y	v	f	t	n	e	b	h	s	q	t	u	g	c
u	z	e	g	w	y	i	x	q	s	j	j	a	d	r
s	z	r	k	y	w	a	m	u	s	e	m	e	n	t

Let's have a test!

1 Which word in this sentence is an antonym of *calm*?

The weather is not as hot and windy today as it was yesterday.

- ◯ weather
- ◯ hot
- ◯ windy
- ◯ yesterday

2 Which pair of words are antonyms?

- ◯ huge, gigantic
- ◯ sink, float
- ◯ guess, estimate
- ◯ argue, squabble

3 Which word in this sentence is a synonym of *daring*?

The racing driver made a bold move to overtake the other cars on the track.

- ◯ racing
- ◯ driver
- ◯ bold
- ◯ track

4 Which pair of words are synonyms?

- ◯ eat, munch
- ◯ walk, crawl
- ◯ cool, comfortable
- ◯ fall, jump

5 Which sentence contains nouns that have been formed from verbs?

- ◯ Multiply them, don't divide them.
- ◯ He is multiplying them, not dividing them.
- ◯ They have been multiplied, not divided.
- ◯ Use multiplication, not division.

6 Which suffix completes the word *punish* correctly in this sentence?

Both boys received the same punish ______________.

- ◯ *ed*
- ◯ *ing*
- ◯ *ment*
- ◯ *dom*

In questions 7–8, choose the word that completes the sentence correctly.

7 They chose that leather for the children's shoes because of its ______________.

- ◯ soften
- ◯ soft
- ◯ softly
- ◯ softness

8 My mother says that I receive a better ______________ than what she did.

- ◯ education
- ◯ educator
- ◯ educated
- ◯ educating

Let's write now!

Create an **advertisement** for a product of your choice. Use **antonyms** to compare your product to others, **synonyms** to add variety to sentences, and **nominalisation** to make some sentences sound more formal.

Glossary of terms

Abbreviations are shortened forms of words or phrases, e.g. RSPCA, Mr.

Adjectives describe **nouns** and **pronouns**. Types of adjectives are:
- **comparing adjectives**, e.g. quieter, quietest
- **descriptive adjectives**, e.g. short, round, little, friendly
- **number adjectives**, e.g. some, many, four.

Adverbs add meaning to verbs by telling how, where, when, how often and to what extent something is done, e.g. quickly, outside, yesterday, always, extremely.

Alliteration is the repetition of consonants in a sequence of words, e.g. a pretty purple parrot.

Antonyms are words that are opposite in meaning, e.g. happy—sad.

Apostrophes are punctuation marks that show:
- where letters are missing when two words are joined to make one shorter word (a contraction), e.g. they're (they are)
- ownership, e.g. Jo's book (the book belonging to Jo).

Articles include the words **a**, **an** and **the**.

Brackets ( ) are punctuation marks containing words that add information to sentences.

Clauses are groups of words that express a complete thought and contain a verb or verb group.

Colons (:) are punctuation marks which show that more information is to follow.

Commas (,) are punctuation marks that:
- separate items in a list
- separate phrases and clauses from the rest of the sentence.

Commands are sentences that tell someone to do something. They usually end with a full stop (.) or sometimes an exclamation mark (!).

Conjunctions are words that connect other words, phrases and clauses in sentences, e.g. and, but, or.

Contractions are words formed when two words are joined to make one, shorter word, e.g. don't (do not).

Exclamations are sentences that express strong feelings. They end with an exclamation mark (!).

Metaphors are figures of speech that directly compare one thing to something else, e.g. The sky is the canopy above my head.

Modality is when verbs and adverbs show how certain we are about something, e.g. might, definitely.

Nominalisation is turning verbs and adjectives into nouns, e.g. excite → excitement.

Nouns are naming words. There are several types of nouns:
- **Abstract nouns** name ideas and feelings, e.g. darkness, happiness.
- **Collective nouns** name groups of people, animals, places or things, e.g. herd, flock.
- **Common nouns** name general people, animals, places or things, e.g. girl, dog, country, car.
- **Compound nouns** are formed by joining two or more words together, e.g. sunlight.
- **Proper nouns** name specific people, animals, places or things, e.g. Tom, Rover, Australia, Halloween.
- **Singular** and **plural nouns**, e.g. book → books.

Onomatopoeia is when words imitate sounds, e.g. Crash!

Phrases are groups of words that do not make sense on their own. They don't usually contain a verb, e.g. in the city, with long hair.

Prepositions are words that connect nouns, pronouns and phrases with other words in a sentence by telling where and when, e.g. in, on, from, since, until.

Pronouns are words that are used in place of nouns. These are:
- **demonstrative pronouns**, e.g. this, those
- **interrogative pronouns**, e.g. Who? What?
- **personal pronouns**, e.g. he, she
- **possessive pronouns**, e.g. his, her
- **reflexive pronouns**, e.g. myself, ourselves
- **relative pronouns**, e.g. that, which.

Questions are sentences that ask for information or opinions. They always end with a question mark (?).

Reported speech tells what other people said, without using their exact words, e.g. He said that he would try to help us.

Rhyme is a pattern of words in poetry that have similar sounds, usually at the ends of lines, e.g. head and read.

Sentences are groups of words that make sense on their own. They always start with a capital letter and can end with a full stop, question mark or exclamation mark.

- **Simple sentences** contain only one verb.
- **Compound sentences** are two simple sentences that are joined together by a conjunction to form a single sentence.
- **Complex sentences** consist of a main clause and one or more dependent clauses.

Similes are figures of speech in which one thing is compared to something unlike itself using the words *like* or *as*, e.g. The lake is like a mirror.

Speech marks are punctuation marks that are placed around spoken language, e.g. "Come here," said Mum.

Statements are sentences that give information or opinions. They always start with a capital letter and end with a full stop.

Subjects are the people, animals or things in a sentence that do the action.

Suffixes are groups of letters attached to the ends of words to change their meaning, e.g. bright, brighter, brightness, brightly.

Synonyms are words that are similar in meaning, e.g. talk, speak.

Tense shows when an action takes place—**present**, **past** or **future**, e.g. walk, walked, will walk.

Verbs are words that show what people, animals or things do. Types of verbs are:

- **being and having verbs**, e.g. is, was, has, had
- **doing verbs**, e.g. run, whispered, thought
- **helping verbs**, e.g. can, will.

Verb groups are groups of words that are built around a verb, e.g. try to catch.

Answers

Unit 1 Wild animals

Let's find them! page 2

1 Cavour Bridge **2** Tiber River **3** Dutch **4** hats **5** Philippines/Mexico **6** grape/grapes **7** clock

Let's go to the next step! page 2

1. In Scotland, New Year is called Hogmanay.
2. Gran always bakes a special cake on New Year's Day.
3. Mum and Dad are going to bring in the New Year in the city.
4. We always bring our dog indoors before the fireworks go off.
5. My teacher, Mr Jones, will be in Singapore on December 31st.
6. We went to their house on Christmas Day and they visited us on New Year's Eve.
7. In some countries in Asia, New Year is sometimes celebrated as late as February.

Let's aim high now! page 2

1. Last year we celebrated Chinese New Year in Shanghai.
2. In some cultures, the first day of the New Year is celebrated in March.
3. There is always a party at the Sydney Opera House on New Year's Eve.
4. The Jewish New Year is called Rosh Hashanah and is celebrated in September.
5. On the stroke of midnight, colourful fireworks burst from the Eiffel Tower in Paris.
6. Places like Auckland, Hong Kong, Beijing and Sydney are among the first to bring in the New Year.
7. My little brother, Tom, has finally worked out that Christmas is exactly seven days before New Year.

Let's find them! page 3

1 crowd **2** heap **3** family **4** celebration **5** entertainment **6** cheer **7** fun

Let's go to the next step! page 4

1. excitement—abstract noun
2. set—collective noun
3. terror—abstract noun
4. wardrobe—collective noun
5. band—collective noun
6. festivities—abstract noun
7. bouquet—collective noun

Let's aim high now! page 4

1. He found information about New Year traditions in the library.
2. The guests of honour arrived at the celebration in a fleet of cars.
3. A galaxy of lights lit up the darkness as the clock struck midnight.
4. I was telling the truth when I said that the orchestra was outstanding.
5. I thought that the troupe of dancers from Brisbane gave the best performance.
6. People were grouped in clusters, waiting to hear the mayor's New Year message.
7. Imagine my amazement when I discovered that I could buy a whole box of fireworks!

Let's put it together now! page 5

Common nouns	Proper nouns	Collective nouns	Abstract nouns	Plural nouns
singer	**audience ✗**	mob	**mosquitoes ✗**	fireworks
stage	London	staff	fun	bodies
building	Eiffel Tower	team	**microphone ✗**	**joy ✗**
costume	New Year's Eve	**London ✗**	joy	mosquitoes
fun ✗	**children ✗**	audience	applause	**Lady Gaga ✗**
microphone	Lady Gaga	orchestra	happiness	children
	Beijing		fright	knives

Let's have fun! page 5

2 bunch (in blue)
3 astonishment (in green)
4 boat (in black)
5 Sydney Harbour Bridge (in red)
6 laughter (in green)
7 fish (in black)
8 Nick (in red)
9 Mandy (in red)

Let's have a test! page 6

1 We spent New Year's Eve in London.
2 The Jacksons may not spend new year in thailand next year.
3 shower
4 curiosity, resolution, tradition, joy
5 The man and woman got home late on New Year's Day.
6 variety
7 thanks
8 festivity

Unit 2 Money

Let's find them! pages 7–8

1 it 2 him 3 Whose 4 them 5 They 6 herself 7 she 8 her

Let's go to the next step! page 8

1 What do they plan to do with all that money?
2 Which of these games are you going to buy?
3 The man said he would use the money to build himself a new house.
4 Mum said she would join me after she had withdrawn money from the ATM.
5 I won't be able to afford the new skateboard unless you lend me some money.
6 I said I would give them an extra five dollars if they helped me clean the garage.
7 He told us that we would be helping ourselves in the future if we started saving money now.

Let's aim high now! page 8

1 Whose—interrogative pronoun
2 me—personal pronoun
3 it—personal pronoun
4 I—personal pronoun
5 Who—interrogative pronoun
6 themselves—reflexive pronoun
7 herself—reflexive pronoun

Let's find them! pages 9–10

1 their 2 her 3 My 4 these 5 your 6 mine 7 our

Let's go to the next step! page 10

1 his 2 her 3 their 4 your 5 hers 6 This 7 those

Let's aim high now! page 10

1 that,his/yours/hers 2 its 3 his/her
4 his/yours/hers 5 These, his/your/my 6 mine
7 his/your/my, that/this

Let's put it together now! page 11

The day of the race finally arrived. Simon checked he's bike again, then placed it carefully on the rack behind they car. Simon was proud of heself because he had found the extra money to pay for the bike. But he knew that if it hadn't been for Grandma, he wouldn't have been able to do it. He looked at hers now and she winked at him. She pointed to her hair, as if to say, "These was you're doing." Whose would have thought he would turn out to be such a good hairdresser?

his, their, himself, her, This, your, Who

Let's have fun! page 11

		1 y	2 o	u	r	3 s	e	l	f	
			u			h				
4 y	o	u	r	s		e			5 t	
o			s						h	
u		6 h	e	r				7 h	e	
			l						i	
			v				8 t		r	
	9 w		e			10 w	h	o	s	e
	11 h	i	s				e			
	a						s			
	12 t	h	a	t		13 w	e			

Let's have a test! page 12

1 us 2 their 3 ourselves 4 What 5 this 6 yours 7 theirs 8 your

Unit 3 Memories

Let's find them! pages 13–14

1 happy **2** plastic **3** northern **4** two **5** several **6** vegemite **7** great

Let's go to the next step! page 14

1 Not <u>all</u> memories are <u>good</u> ones.
2 I love looking at the <u>old</u> photographs in Mum's <u>big</u>, <u>wooden</u> chest.
3 I have <u>many</u> memories of the time we spent with a <u>Chinese</u> family.
4 I remember when Grandpa gave me <u>six little toy</u> cars for my birthday.
5 My mother reminded me that I was also <u>scared</u> on my <u>first</u> day at school.
6 The <u>large</u> photograph in the <u>silver</u> frame is of my dad and me on our <u>last</u> <u>fishing</u> trip.
7 When I saw the <u>colourful</u> postcard, it brought back <u>pleasant</u> memories of our <u>African</u> safari.

Let's aim high now! page 14

1 straight **2** rough **3** cheap **4** terrible **5** boring **6** worthless **7** clear

Let's find them! pages 15–16

1 more interesting **2** brighter **3** bigger **4** better **5** best **6** oldest **7** biggest **8** more important

Let's go to the next step! page 16

Adjective	Comparative	Superlative
happy	happier	happiest
exciting	more exciting	most exciting
dangerous	**more dangerous**	**most dangerous**
easy	**easier**	**easiest**
pretty	**prettier**	**prettiest**
brave	**braver**	**bravest**
beautiful	**more beautiful**	**most beautiful**
lucky	**luckier**	**luckiest**
curious	**more curious**	**most curious**
large	**larger**	**largest**
tall	**taller**	**tallest**
peaceful	**more peaceful**	**most peaceful**
busy	**busier**	**busiest**
young	**younger**	**youngest**

Let's aim high now! page 16

1 worst **2** better **3** shortest **4** most playful **5** clearer **6** bigger **7** most incredible

Let's put it together now! page 17

I have the <u>more brilliant</u> memories of the time we spent in the <u>Australia</u> outback last year. We travelled through a <u>widest</u> variety of landscapes, from <u>dustier</u> plains to <u>rockiest</u> mountain ranges, and each one seemed <u>beautifuller</u> than the last. It was definitely the <u>good</u> holiday I've ever had!
<u>most brilliant</u>, <u>Australian</u>, <u>wide</u>, <u>dusty</u>, <u>rocky</u>, <u>more beautiful</u>, <u>best</u>

Let's have fun! page 17

O	L	D	E	R					
D	E	L	I	G	H	T	F	U	L
H	E	L	P	F	U	L			
N	E	W							
H	A	P	P	I	E	S	T		
B	E	S	T						
D	E	L	I	C	I	O	U	S	
B	R	I	G	H	T				

Let's have a test! page 18

1 several
2 forgetful
3 This little red Chinese lantern reminds me of my holiday.
4 hopeful
5 than
6 the worst
7 further
8 the most difficult

Unit 4 Video and computer games

Let's find them! page 20

2 develop—present tense
3 have—present tense
4 will look—future tense
5 were—past tense
6 used—past tense
7 love—present tense

Let's go to the next step! page 20

Present tense	Past tense	Future tense
compete	competed	will compete
buy	**bought**	**will buy**
make	**made**	will make
watch	**watched**	**will watch**
control	controlled	**will control**
move	**moved**	will move
win	**won**	**will win**
complete	**completed**	will complete
allow	**allowed**	will allow
eat	**ate**	**will eat**

Let's aim high now! page 20

1 are **2** is **3** will play **4** had **5** beats **6** showed **7** will take

Let's find them! pages 21–22

1. The player must move Pac-Man through a maze of dots.
2. If Pac-Man can eat all the dots, the player moves to the next level.
3. When the player has lost three lives, the game is over.
4. The player must earn points.
5. When a ghost has been eaten, its eyes return to the centre of the screen.
6. If a player manages to get 10 000 points, they get a bonus life.
7. The first person to reach that score was from Florida.

Let's go to the next step! page 22

1 could/must/should **2** have **3** must/should **4** could/should **5** are **6** am **7** has

Let's aim high now! page 22

1 has destroyed **2** might buy **3** will get **4** does play **5** are aiming **6** could play **7** have done

Let's put it together now page 23

was launched
has four modes
must **race**
has to finish
lose
that **is** left
hope there **will/are going to** be

Let's have fun! page 23

1 sat **2** could **3** clapped **4** were **5** heard **6** came **7** began **8** struck **9** said **10** broke

Answer: Super Mario

Let's have a test! page 24

1 tries **2** is **3** had **4** will get **5** should have **6** to play **7** would have played **8** should have won

Unit 5 Optical illusions

Let's find them! page 25

1 verb **2** verb **3** adjective **4** adjective **5** adjective **6** verb

Let's go to the next step! page 26

1 flying **2** haunted **3** exciting **4** howling **5** sinking **6** roasted **7** sloping

Let's aim high now! page 26

1 leaking **2** boiled **3** knitted **4** talking **5** entertaining **6** chopped **7** crumpled

Let's find them! page 27

1 Creating **2** folding **3** Using **4** measuring **5** marking **6** looking **7** seeing **8** believing

Let's go to the next step! page 28

1 Looking **2** Performing **3** following **4** cheering **5** ringing **6** queuing **7** murmuring

Let's aim high now! page 28

1. The magician created the illusion by using a set of mirrors.
2. Sitting in the front row, I could see exactly what the illusionist was doing.
3. The trick failed because of the illusionist's fumbling.
4. The illusionist distracted the audience by telling them a joke
5. The magician showed us the trick without revealing his secret.
6. I have learnt how to create an illusion by hiding a card up my sleeve.
7. After practising for hours every day, they finally mastered the trick.

Let's put it together now! page 29

Making
interesting
coloured
Using
completed
taping
spinning

Let's have fun! page 29

x	s	t	v	a	n	i	s	h	i	n	g	v	a	o
c	i	x	v	w	q	h	y	h	o	p	p	i	n	g
h	t	b	a	s	s	q	j	f	n	d	z	n	f	d
d	t	j	g	n	i	y	l	f	h	e	r	d	j	k
l	i	r	w	c	n	w	f	h	j	h	z	e	m	o
e	n	q	v	a	q	r	h	j	d	s	h	t	i	k
h	g	t	i	h	g	f	h	s	h	i	g	n	g	d
a	f	j	n	n	z	x	n	v	s	n	w	i	r	t
g	n	i	h	c	t	a	w	h	h	i	k	a	c	x
a	f	e	y	u	w	y	u	h	k	f	b	p	b	p
z	y	r	d	e	k	o	o	c	i	p	u	h	d	a

Let's have a test! page 30

1 amazing **2** scared **3** boring **4** missing
5 Waiting **6** Watching **7** swimming **8** Waving

Unit 6 Fables

Let's find them! page 32

2 place **3** manner **4** frequency **5** manner
6 degree **7** frequency

Let's go to the next step! page 32

1 yesterday **2** sadly **3** brightly **4** away **5** hardly
6 Lately, properly **7** seldom

Let's aim high now! page 32

1. The wolf eyed the sheep greedily. manner
2. The girl left the book of fables here. place
3. The boy knew that there was a wolf nearby. place
4. The shepherd ran enthusiastically to his flock. manner
5. The boy immediately ran to warn the villagers. time
6. I have almost finished reading the book of fables. degree
7. The fable teaches us that people never listen to a liar. frequency

Let's find them! pages 33–34

2. describing an adjective
3. describing another adverb
4. comparing two ways of doing something
5. describing an adjective
6. describing an adjective
7. describing another adverb

Let's go to the next step! page 34

1. (~~near~~/nearly)
2. (~~most~~/almost)
3. (really/~~real~~)
4. (~~more certainly~~/most certainly)
5. (~~to~~/too/~~two~~)
6. (~~cleverly~~/more cleverly)
7. (~~easier~~/more easily)

Let's aim high now! page 34

1 closer **2** often **3** carefully **4** stupidly
5 extremely **6** fairly **7** confidently

Let's put it together now! page 35

One day a tortoise challenged a hare to a race. The hare thought the tortoise was being utter ridiculous and laughed loud. Nevertheless, he accepted the tortoise's challenge and the two lined up. The hare, who could run much fastest than the tortoise, raced ahead. He got so further ahead of the tortoise that he decided to have a nap, believing that he would still have lots of time to get to the finish line before his rival. But the hare slept most deeply than he expected, and while he was sleeping, the tortoise plodded on steady. When the hare woke up, the tortoise was nearing the finish line. The hare tried to catch up, but the tortoise beat him easy.

utterly, loudly, faster, far, more deeply, steadily, easily

Let's have fun page 35

slowly
Sometimes
mostly
always
angrily
very
quite
soon

Let's have a test! page 36

1 The girl frequently reads the book of fables.
2 I have read this fable before.
3 The wolf is watching nearby.
4 The sheep bleated helplessly.
5 hardly
6 extremely
7 more heavily
8 most likely

Unit 7 Inventions that have changed the way we live

Let's find them! page 37

1 from 2 for 3 of 4 without 5 during
6 before

Let's go to the next step! page 38

1 since 2 by 3 to 4 beside, on 5 about, in
6 before 7 above

Let's aim high now! page 38

1 (~~to~~, of, about) 2 (for, from, ~~of~~) 3 (on, ~~of~~, off)
4 (under, on, ~~in~~) 5 (~~in~~, up, down)
6 (~~by~~, through, out)
7 (by, ~~between~~, past) / (to, on, ~~of~~)

Let's find them! page 39

1 when 2 where 3 how often 4 when 5 why
6 where 7 when

Let's go to the next step page 40

1 I amazed everyone with my new invention.
2 He goes to his laboratory as often as possible.
3 In the future, someone might invent a flying car.
4 The inventor has a laboratory behind his house.
5 The instrument she invented works better than his.
6 We saw the latest gadgets at the International Inventors' Fair.
7 When my dad test-drove the new car, he wanted it more than ever.

Let's aim high now! page 40

1 in the rubbish bin where
2 for hours on end to what extent
3 without difficulty how
4 onto the stage where
5 with much greater speed how
6 now and again how often
7 at about six o'clock when

Let's put it together now! page 41

Bicycles have had a huge impact in people's lives since they were first invented on the 19th century. In some countries, they are still the main form off transport, while in others they are used mainly from recreation. The first two-wheel vehicle was invented about the German, Baron Karl Vondrais. The wheels, which weren't the same size, were attached towards a wooden frame. The bicycle didn't have pedals. The rider had to push the bicycle forward without his feet.
on, in, of, for, by, to, with

Let's have fun! page 41

				[1] i	n	s	i	d	e						
				n										[2] u	[3] p
				[4] t	o	[5] w	a	r	[6] d	s					a
[7] b				o		i			o						s
e						[8] t	o		[9] w	i	t	h	[10] o	u	t
[11] t	h	r	o	u	g	h			n				v		
w													e		
e			[12] a	t					[13] u	n	[14] d	e	r		
e			c					[15] r			u				
[16] n	e	a	r					o			r				
			[17] o	f	[18] f			[19] u	n	t	i	l			
			s		r			n			n				
			s		o			d			g				
					m										

Let's have a test! page 42

1 I left my invention at school.
2 to
3 for
4 for
5 early in the morning
6 since last year
7 past the sun came up
8 to the park

Unit 8 Food from around the world

Let's find them! pages 43–44

1 in a traditional Thai sarong
2 next to the window
3 of water
4 on the menu
5 with noodles

6 inside the spring rolls
7 in a tall glass

Let's go to the next step! page 44

1 I prefer eating fruits without seeds.
2 The chef uses coriander from his garden.
3 Thai food is a mixture of different flavours.
4 The chef in the tall hat makes amazing food.
5 The bottle behind the vinegar contains fish sauce.
6 The restaurant down the road makes delicious spring rolls.
7 The customers near the window have ordered Tom Yum Soup.

Let's aim high now! page 44

1 of chocolates
2 in the pot
3 serving the food
4 covered in sauce
5 on the tables
6 with deep pockets
7 at the Chinese restaurant

Let's find them! pages 45–46

1 To make this dish, you will need lots of ingredients.
2 The recipe uses minced beef, spaghetti sauce and an egg.
3 It also uses breadcrumbs, garlic, salt, cheese and spaghetti.
4 Prepare the spaghetti, following the directions on the packet.
5 In a large bowl, combine the remaining ingredients.
6 After that, place the meatballs in the sauce.
7 When cooked, serve the meatballs and sauce over the spaghetti.

Let's go to the next step! page 46

1 I had sushi, an apple and a fruit drink for lunch.
2 You can buy pizzas in supermarkets, bakeries and restaurants.
3 The vegetables on my plate were green, orange, red and yellow.
4 There were knives, forks, spoons, plates and glasses on the table.
5 The chef peeled the potatoes, chopped the vegetables and prepared the sauce.
6 I helped Mum by setting the table, packing away the dishes and making the tea.
7 The restaurant was decorated with little fountains, statues and paintings of people eating.

Let's aim high now! page 46

1 To my horror, they offered me stink bugs to eat!
2 Without a doubt, the food from Korea is the tastiest.
3 They used vegetables, herbs and spices in that dish.
4 Some people don't like ice-cream, chocolate or cake!
5 I have eaten food from Italy, Greece, Vietnam and China.
6 I never add salt, pepper, vinegar or tomato sauce to my food.
7 Thai food, with its mixture of delicious flavours, is very popular.

Let's put it together now page 47

Italian food, with its rich flavours and fresh ingredients, is enjoyed by men, women and children all over the world. The most popular foods from Italy are pasta, pizza and different types of cheeses. Customers **in/at** Italian restaurants usually order pasta or pizza. Italian restaurants also serve lots **of** gelato. Of all the different types of food, I like Italian food the best!

Let's have fun! page 47

1 chefs from France
lettuce on a salad sandwich
pizza in the wood—fired oven
gelato from the freezer
dessert with cream topping
sausages on the barbecue
2 To complete this dish, I still need to add the herbs, adjust the seasoning and heat it through.
I will finish off the dessert with a swirl of cream, shaved chocolate, nuts and a cherry.

Let's have a test! page 48

1 A chef from a famous restaurant is preparing our meal.
2 with chillies
3 without sauce
4 on the bakery
5 a pie, mashed potatoes and gravy
6 I like Italian food, Chinese food and Mexican food.

7 I like many Mexican dishes, especially the very spicy ones.

8 In some countries, such as China, Korea and Japan, people use chopsticks.

Unit 9 Safety rules!

Let's find them! pages 49–50

1 statement 2 question 3 question 4 statement 5 question 6 statement 7 question

Let's go to the next step! page 50

2 I cut it while I was chopping the carrots.
3 I don't want to spread germs and diseases.
4 I moved it away from the heater.
5 I won't let you stay at home alone.
6 You should learn how to swim.
7 He's going to use the leaf blower.

Let's aim high now! page 50

1 Has the girl had a bad accident?
2 Can roller skates be dangerous?
3 Will she be more careful in future?
4 Is she teaching him how to swim?
5 Has he worn safety glasses before?
6 Were the cyclists putting on their helmets?
7 Should he change the battery in the fire alarm?

Let's find them! page 51

1 command 2 exclamation 3 command 4 exclamation 5 command 6 exclamation 7 command

Let's go to the next step! page 52

1 Throw 2 Switch 3 Wear 4 Stay 5 Hold 6 Keep 7 Drive

Let's aim high now! page 52

1 pain 2 sympathy 3 anger 4 disgust 5 disbelief 6 delight 7 admiration

Let's put it together now! page 53

What are you doing, Dad?
I'm changing the batteries in the smoke alarm.
Are you sure that ladder is safe, Dad?
It's fine./! Pass me that battery.
That ladder looks really rickety, Dad.
I told you, it's fine./!
Oh, my back!

Let's have fun! page 53

Frame 1: Mum says: Be careful!
Frame 2: Mum says: What a mess!
Frame 3: Mum says: Have you cleaned up yet?
Frame 4: Boy says: I'm doing it now, Mum.

Let's have a test! page 54

1 That ride is dangerous.
2 How many times has he fallen?
3 Should
4 What
5 Keep away from the building site!
6 How
7 Go
8 That dog has very big teeth!

Unit 10 Digging up the past

Let's find them! pages 55–56

1 Pompeii in Italy is one of the most famous archeological sites in the world.
2 Excavations on the site started about 250 years ago.
3 They continue to this day.
4 Archeologists discovered the outlines of 2000 bodies.
5 They also found bread in an oven!
6 Pompeii is one of Italy's most popular tourist destinations.
7 More than two million people visit it every year!

Let's go to the next step! page 56

The **incorrect** verbs are:

1 have been 2 are learning 3 has been 4 are finding 5 is eating 6 were looking 7 was watching

Let's aim high now! page 56

1 Artifacts from Pompeii include frescoes, coins and statues.
2 The archeologist is working on a new dig.
3 Everyone on the dig shares the archeologist's enthusiasm.
4 The tourists were looking forward to their visit to Pompeii.
5 The documentary was about the destruction of Pompeii.

6 The books in the library contain pictures of archeological digs.

7 The archeological dig is a fascinating place.

Let's find them! pages 57–58

1 Thousands of statues have been unearthed, yet no two are alike. (compound sentence)

2 Some are marching and others are kneeling. (compound sentence)

3 The list goes on. (simple sentence)

4 The statues form part of the tomb of the first emperor of China and are in underground trenches. (compound sentence)

5 In some of the trenches there are clay horses with wooden chariots behind them. (simple sentence)

6 Archeologists have found swords and other weapons in some trenches. (simple sentence)

Let's go to the next step! page 58

1 The molten ash covered the people and they died instantly.

2 The archeologist knew the area well, yet she got lost.

3 Many of the residents of Pompeii were killed, but some escaped.

4 Mount Vesuvius could erupt at any time, so it is still a threat.

5 The archeologist might be at the dig, or she might be in the museum.

6 I have seen Pompeii, but I haven't seen the terracotta warriors.

7 My mother is interested in archeology, so she organised a visit to a dig.

Let's aim high now! page 58

1 He is an archeologist, **but/yet** he has never worked on a dig.

2 The bus was going to Pompeii, **so** the tourists climbed aboard.

3 The children found some coins in the field, **but** they weren't very old.

4 The shards of pottery are the same colour, **but/yet** they don't belong together.

5 They might be a dinosaur's bones, **or** they might be a mammoth's bones.

6 I went to an archeological site, he went to a museum **and** she visited the caves.

7 The statue was made of marble, the jar was made of clay **and** the plate was made of silver.

Let's put it together now! page 59

Stonehenge in England **is** almost 5000 years old. Archeologists have studied the site**,** they have dug up artifacts **and** they have unearthed an ancient village nearby. But Stonehenge's past remains a mystery. Experts do have some ideas about what Stonehenge may have been used for. Ancient people may have used it as an observatory**, or** it may have been a cemetery. Archeologists are still searching for answers to Stonehenge's past**, but/yet** they are no closer to finding them.

Let's have fun! page 59

Simple sentence: An archeologist is inspecting the coins.

Compound sentence: The archeologists are talking and the students are listening.

Let's have a test! page 60

1 The statues 2 The books 3 is counting
4 are helping 5 and 6 or 7 , or 8 , but

Unit 11 Insects with dirty habits

Let's find them! page 62

1 Although 2 as 3 Once 4 When 5 If 6 that
7 which 8 so

Let's go to the next step! page 62

1 The flies won't get onto the meat if you cover it.

2 When we went to China, we saw lots of dried dung beetles.

3 I've learnt a lot about dung beetles since I last saw you.

4 I watched in fascination as the dung beetle rolled its ball of dung over the anthill.

5 Dung beetles are sometimes called rollers because they roll dung into balls.

6 The scarab beetle, which is a type of dung beetle, was once thought to be sacred.

7 Our soil will continue to deteriorate, unless we bring more dung beetles into the country.

Let's aim high now! page 62

1 There are lots of scientists in the world who study dung beetles.

2 I became interested in dung beetles when I saw one in our garden.

3 We went to a temple in Egypt where we saw images of scarab beetles.

4 Although I'd seen many pictures of dung beetles, I'd never seen a real one until today.
5 Mum made me wash my hands after I'd handled the dung ball.
6 Wherever we went on the farm, we saw dung beetles.
7 The dung beetle kept on trying until it got the dung ball over the rise.

Let's find them! page 63

1 After being submerged in water for half an hour, they are able to recover.
2 Some experts even say that if there is a nuclear explosion, cockroaches will survive.
3 And although they prefer warm climates, they can live in freezing temperatures.
4 When exposed to light, they run away.
5 This also makes it difficult to get rid of them, as they are so hard to find.
6 An exception is the Asian cockroach, which is attracted to light.
7 Because cockroaches are a danger to our health, we should try to keep them out of our homes.

Let's go to the next step! page 64

1 When I looked in the box, I saw two cockroaches.
2 Although I can't see the cockroach, I know it's there.
3 While you search for the cockroach, I'll empty the bins.
4 If you don't want cockroaches eating your food, cover it.
5 The cockroach, which was enormous, was staring at me.
6 Whenever my little sister sees a cockroach, she screams.
7 The scientist, who has spent years studying cockroaches, will retire soon.

Let's aim high now! page 64

1 Although I hear cockroaches, I never see them.
2 The boy, whose mum works with mine, collects cockroaches!
3 Before we moved into the house, we checked for cockroaches.
4 The world's biggest cockroach, which is found in Australia, is 9cm long.
5 While dung beetles help humans, cockroaches are of no use to them.
6 I don't like cockroaches, mainly because they can spread diseases.
7 When they checked out of the hotel, they complained about the cockroaches.

Let's put it together now! page 65

Wherever there are people, there are flies. The house fly, which makes up about 90% of all domestic flies, is the most widely distributed of all insects. Because it can carry serious diseases, it is considered a pest. The female lays about 500 eggs and within a day, the larvae, known as maggots, hatch. After they have gorged themselves on dead and decaying matter, they become pupae. The adult flies emerge from the pupae. Adult flies, which are 8–12mm long, live for between two weeks and a month.

Let's have fun! page 65

n	e	v	s	s	e	l	n	u	b	m	i
w	c	h	g	r	q	x	b	d	y	o	p
a	n	f	c	o	c	k	r	o	a	c	h
t	i	v	e	j	k	q	b	n	r	q	c
c	s	r	t	a	h	t	u	w	a	b	x
i	v	r	s	w	t	k	a	f	t	e	r
f	p	n	m	s	a	z	z	w	q	g	y
w	c	e	o	x	g	e	r	u	y	l	f
d	b	h	q	b	e	r	q	x	b	s	z
u	e	w	o	v	y	e	b	d	m	v	s
n	t	t	y	q	p	h	u	n	t	i	l
g	i	o	h	w	a	w	n	q	w	x	z

Let's have a test! page 66

1 The girl, whose father is an entomologist, knows a lot about insects.
2 that
3 while
4 because
5 Although cockroaches are pests, I am not frightened of them.
6 The dung beetle, which was burying its dung, was attacked by a bird.
7 , whereas
8 , which

Unit 12 Strange, but true

Let's find them! page 67

1 The croc **2** the crocodile **3** The phone **4** Vets **5** Crocs

Let's go to the next step! page 68

1 that **2** who **3** that **4** who/that **5** whose **6** which **7** which

Let's aim high now! page 68

1 that my brother caught
2 whom I interviewed
3 whose favourite food is meat
4 who sits next to me
5 which is a crowded city
6 which had been missing for four years
7 that I read in a science magazine

Let's find them! pages 69–70

2 a small, unlocked window
3 His only option
4 an uncomfortable six hours
5 the help of the fire department
6 The burglar, who was not allowed to speak to us,
7 The owner of the house

Let's go to the next step! page 70

1 I read the story about the burglar yesterday.
2 The pizza, which was huge, fed fifty people!
3 My brother's dog has short legs and a long tail.
4 The old lady, who loves animals, has sixteen cats!
5 The little girl in the pink dress can juggle five balls!
6 I saw a cockroach without a head running across the room.
7 Some spectators at the cricket match were wearing strange outfits.

Let's aim high now! page 70

1 your heart
2 a book about strange events
3 Sneezing with your eyes open
4 its own strange stories
5 The burglar who got stuck in a window
6 a python that is six metres long
7 The shop, which has just opened,

Let's put it together now! page 71

Some people have names **that** cause them problems. **Poor** Stan Still doesn't know what to do when people say, "Stan Still! Get a move on!" A website, **which** recently conducted a survey of people's names, found that many parents don't think of the problems that unusual names could cause for their children. There are people **whose** parents have called their sons Chris when their surname is Cross, and their daughters Paige when their surname is Turner. And then there's Mr Hole, **who** is stuck with the name Doug. **A** spokesperson for the website said, "Think before you choose a name for **your** child. If your surname is Case, don't call your child Justin or Justine."

Let's have fun! page 71

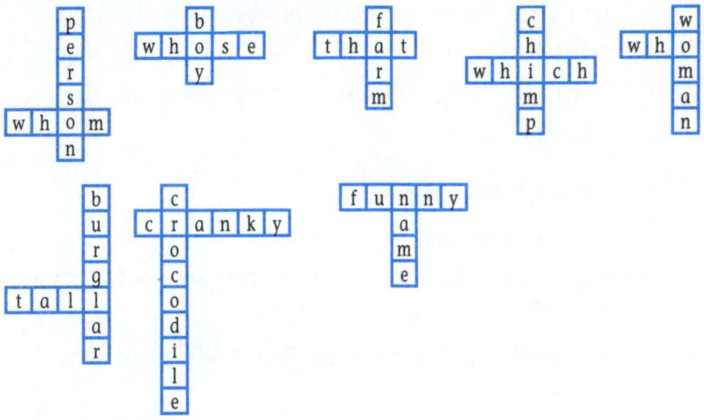

Let's have a test! page 72

1 This story, which comes from Spain, is strange.
2 was
3 who told us the story
4 that is flying backwards
5 a tall, thin
6 Two very big crocodiles
7 an small window
8 A experienced zookeeper

Unit 13 Australian artists

Let's find them! pages 73–74

1 He learnt skills such as carpentry and sheep shearing while he lived on a mission station.
2 However, after studying the works of the artists Rex Battarbee and John Gardner, Albert started painting his own landscapes.
3 When Battarbee saw Albert's talent, he offered to give him lessons.

4 He was awarded the Queen's Coronation Medal in 1953 and was presented to Queen Elizabeth when she came to Australia the following year.

5 Although Albert died in 1959, his paintings remain popular.

Let's go to the next step! page 74

1 If 2 since 3 until 4 Whenever 5 because
6 although 7 unless

Let's aim high now! page 74

2 As soon as I saw the painting, I knew who the artist was.

3 The artist takes her sketchpad with her wherever she goes.

4 We'll stay at the art gallery until it closes.

5 When we get to the art gallery, you can look at whatever you wish.

6 I don't like those paintings because they are very dull.

7 We'll go to the café once we've seen all the paintings.

Let's find them! pages 75–76

1 I'm not really sure ... except

2 Alison: Did anyone encourage you to become an artist?

3 Margaret: (without hesitation) My mother!

4 Well ... I suppose

5 Her motto was: if you want to do something, do it!

6 I paint what's around me (gesturing at the objects in the room).

Let's go to the next step! page 76

1 I was thinking ... no, that wouldn't work.

2 Pablo Picasso (1881–1973) is a very famous artist.

3 Let's see ... you could paint those hills a lighter colour.

4 I've visited galleries on many continents: Europe, America and Australia.

5 Albert Namatjira was born on a mission station in the Northern Territory (NT).

6 The artist has collected many objects: old tyres, bits of steel and balls of string.

7 Which of these canvases should I use: the square one or the rectangular one?

Let's aim high now! page 76

1 I think I'll put my paintbrushes away ... or maybe I won't.

2 That painting is ... now what's the word I'm looking for?

3 You'll never believe where we went today: to the art gallery!

4 Albert Namatjira (born Elea Namatjira) was a very successful artist.

5 I've drawn up a list of the items I need: paints, brushes and an easel.

6 Albert Namatjira (1902–1959) painted landscapes of the Australian outback.

7 The artist finds inspiration everywhere: at home, in the city and in the country.

Let's put it together now! page 77

Sidney Nolan (1917–1992) is an important Australian artist. This is my imaginary interview with him.

Kathy: Good morning, Sidney.

Sidney: Good morning.

Kathy: I'd like to start by asking you about your Ned Kelly paintings.

Sidney: (looks amused) Yes, I thought you might.

Kathy: They're still very popular. Why do you think that is?

Sidney: Mmm ... that's a difficult question to answer. I think it's **because** I've used strong, simple lines. They look a bit like children's art. People seem to like that.

Kathy: Did you enjoy painting them?

Sidney: Well ... yes and no. **Although** they are popular today, I wasn't sure at the time that people would like them./They are popular today, **but** I wasn't sure at the time that people would like them.

Let's have fun page 77

1 rainbow 2 sun 3 water

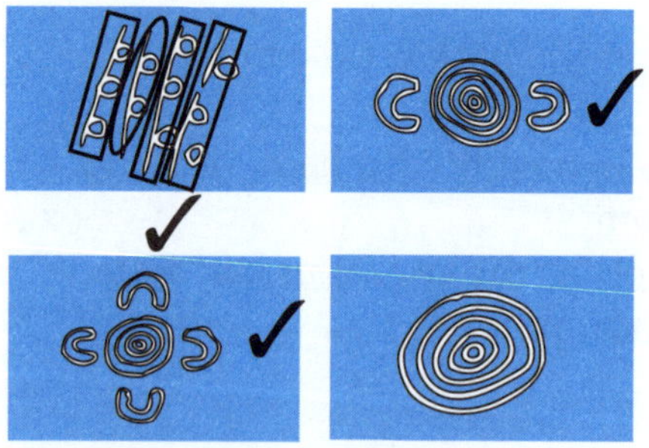

Let's have a test! page 78

1 since

2 because

3 while

4 Although I did not like the painting, I bought it.

5 We walked into the gallery and ... there it was!

6 Artworld (the gallery's magazine) comes out once a month.

7 These are the things I like to paint: mountains, trees and rivers.

8 I have an announcement to make: the painting sold for $10 million!

Unit 14 Recycling

Let's find them! pages 79–80

1 high 2 high 3 low 4 low 5 low 6 high 7 high

Let's go to the next step! page 80

1 I always put my rubbish in the right bin.

2 We may produce less rubbish in the future.

3 One day they might be able to recycle plastic bags.

4 You must not put your old clothes in the recycling bin.

5 He never puts his scraps of paper in the recycling bin.

6 Recycling is something we should all be taking seriously.

7 Perhaps more people will start recycling and reusing things.

Let's aim high now! page 80

1 perhaps 2 should 3 might 4 never/always 5 definitely 6 always/never 7 must

Let's find them! page 81

1 Ave 2 Mr 3 e.g. 4 Dr 5 Australia 6 Victoria 7 New South Wales

Let's go to the next step! page 82

1 ~~klm~~/km 2 Rd/~~R~~ 3 ~~tele~~/TV 4 ~~Mnt~~/Mt 5 Aug/~~Au~~ 6 m/~~met~~ 7 ~~Pof~~/PO

Let's aim high now! page 82

1 north-east 2 Crescent 3 Department 4 university 5 United Nations 6 Professor 7 Member of Parliament

Let's put it together now! page 83

We **must** all try to reuse or recycle things as much as possible. If you have old towels or blankets, the **RSPCA** will **definitely** take them. You **could** also take your old ink cartridges to the shop next to **St** Mark's College. And **never** throw away clothes and toys that are still in good condition. Let someone else enjoy them. To find a charity near you that you can donate them to, go to **www**.auscharity.org.

Let's have fun page 83

1 might 2 perhaps 3 surely 4 may 5 should 6 will 7 always

Medical supplies—Dr

Army supplies—Capt.

An uncle in Christchurch—NZ

Friends in America—US

Relations in England—UK

A cousin in Darwin—NT

The lady of the house—Mrs

An important person—VIP

Let's have a test! page 84

1 will 2 can't, might 3 probably 4 must 5 kg 6 PS 7 tsp 8 am

Unit 15 Best sellers

Let's find them! page 86

1 He's 2 she's 3 He'd 4 doesn't 5 There's 6 that's 7 I've

Let's go to the next step! page 86

1 This term we're reading a book that's on the best seller list.

2 They're discussing the book that they've just finished reading.

3 I'll give the book to my friend to read when I've finished with it.

4 I would've finished the book sooner if I'd had more time to read it.

5 I couldn't find the book in the library so I haven't finished my project.

6 I don't want to read that book because my friend says it isn't interesting.

7 He won't read this book because someone told him it's got scary parts in it.

Let's aim high now! page 86

1 Who is going to be the first one to read this book? Who's

2 You should not force people to read books they do not like. shouldn't, don't

3 They will hear the authors speak about their books at the book fair. They'll

4 You must not read that book as it is not suitable for young children. mustn't, isn't

5 This author is an amazing writer and I intend reading all of his books. author's

6 I have not read any of this author's books, but I believe they are very good. haven't, they're

7 They said they would try to find the book, but they were not sure if it was still in print. they'd, weren't

Let's find them! page 87

1 people **2** Afghanistan **3** Jamal **4** his mum **5** the soldiers **6** the smugglers **7** the parents

Let's go to the next step! page 88

1. Those bookcases' shelves need to be fixed.
2. I like the look of this book's cover, so I might read it.
3. This is the tenth week that the author's new book has been on the best seller list.
4. I found this book in the children's section, but I think it belongs with the adults' books.
5. This story's ending is very sad, unlike the other stories' endings, which are much happier.
6. They announced the book of the year after counting both the critics' votes and the people's votes.
7. Some students in our class are going to the writers' festival, which is being held in the city's largest conference centre.

Let's aim high now! page 88

1. the illustrator's name
2. the writer's words
3. The novel's plot
4. The bookshop's shelves
5. Certain authors' works
6. the characters' backgrounds
7. JRR Tolkien's books

Let's put it together now! page 89

One of my favourite **books** is Gillian **Rubinstein's** science fiction novel *Space Demons*. **It's** about a group of children who get sucked into a computer game and have to fight their way out of it. The **characters'** true personalities are revealed by the way they act once **they're** inside the game. The more hateful their thoughts, the harder it is to break the **game's** hold on them. **I'm** not a great fan of computer games, but I really enjoyed this book, and I think you will too.

Let's have fun page 89

1 doesn't **2** you're **3** I'm **4** author's **5** it's **6** novels' **7** they're **8** isn't **9** book's **10** children's

Let's have a test! page 90

1. Max doesn't know what the book is about.
2. you're, you'll
3. It's, its
4. We are
5. book's pages
6. people's
7. woman's
8. books, year's

Unit 16 Where does it come from?

Let's find them! page 92

1. "It's an apple," she said, and carried on reading.
2. "Mandy, Mandy," Tom continued, "do you know where it comes from?"
3. "But where did it come from before that, Mandy?" Tom asked.
4. "Now leave me alone, I'm trying to read."
5. "Where did the apple tree come from, Mandy?" persisted Tom.
6. "It comes from a seed," she said, more kindly this time.
7. "But where does the seed come from, Mandy?"

Let's go to the next step! page 92

1. Mum said, "I didn't know that cork comes from oak trees."
2. "I thought these oranges were from Queensland," said Joel.
3. "Look at this beautiful outfit," said Aunt Sarah. "I got it in Paris!"
4. "Most of the films in our cinemas come from America," said Chrissy.
5. "I've found out where this necklace comes from!" exclaimed Ramina.
6. "Grandma says these silver candlesticks come from Russia," said Ursula.
7. "Mum says I get my good looks from her and my brains from Dad!" announced Cindy.

Let's aim high now! page 92

1 "Where did all this water come from?" asked Mum.
2 "Which animal do these horns come from?" asked Lara.
3 "Thousands of items are made from oil," explained our science teacher.
4 "These tusks," said the lady at the museum, "are from a woolly mammoth."
5 "Today we learnt that butter and cheese come from milk," said the little boy.
6 "May I hand out the souvenirs I got for everyone while I was in Japan?" asked Zac.
7 "Divers have found a shipwreck dating from the 1st century," announced the newsreader.

Let's find them! page 93

1 Mum asked him what he was doing.
2 He said he was digging a hole.
3 She asked him why he was burying his apple.
4 Tom said he was growing an apple tree.
5 He announced proudly that he'd worked it all out.
6 Mum said that it wasn't that simple.
7 He said that if Mandy said that was what happened, it must be true!

Let's go to the next step! page 94

Correct options:

1 had 2 were 3 would 4 knew 5 didn't, had
6 was 7 should, had

Let's aim high now! page 94

1 He said that the milk was from the farm.
2 Mr Norton said that he knew where to find the picture.
3 The man said that the noise was coming from the roof.
4 The lady said that she had no idea which book the recipe was from.
5 Mrs Caro said that the dance troupe came from Russia.
6 The man said that he would try to find out where the rabbit's burrow was.
7 The lady from the weather bureau warned that cold weather was coming from the south.

Let's put it together now! page 95

"I bet you don't know where milk comes from," said Milly.
"Yes I do!" replied Sam indignantly, "it comes from the supermarket!"
"No it doesn't," said Milly, "it comes from a cow."
"Oh that's really silly, Milly," said Sam. "I've never seen a cow in the supermarket before."
Milly **told** Sam that he didn't know anything, but Sam said he obviously **knew** more than Milly about where milk came from.

Let's have fun page 95

1 "It comes from Ancient Egypt," replied Suzy.
2 "He comes from a well-known fairy tale," answered Tom.
3 "It comes from Taronga Zoo in Sydney," said Tim.
4 Joanne said that it came from the queen's crown.
5 Mum said that it came from the bakery down the road.

Let's have a test! page 96

1 "The cyclist came from nowhere," said the driver.
2 "I don't know where Grandma got this locket," said Mum, "or these rings."
3 ?
4 !
5 My friend asked me if I knew where the new boy came from.
6 that
7 didn't, had
8 shouldn't

Unit 17 Colours

Let's find them! page 98

Similes: Green is … as graceful as the trees when they start to sway/as fresh as the grass which has just been mown/as bright as the leaves which are newly grown
White is … like the ash when the fire dies/like the snow—crisp and cold/like our hair when we grow old
Metaphors: The lake is the mirror that reflects my smiles/This book is a memory of words that I've read
Rhyming words: day and sway/eyes and

dies/cold and old/head and read/smiles and trials

Let's go to the next step! page 98

1 metaphor **2** simile **3** metaphor **4** simile
5 rhyming words **6** rhyming words

Let's aim high now! page 98

1 white **2** orange **3** green **4** gold **5** red **6** sight
7 shampoo

Let's find them! page 99

Onomatopoeia: beep-beep-beeping/ swishing/squeals/screeching/crunch/squawks/ rustling
Alliteration: **b**eep-**b**eep-**b**eeping of my **b**lue/ **s**wishing in the kitchen **s**ink/**s**ister's **s**queals/ **s**creeching **s**iren/**b**ig **b**lack

Let's go to the next step! page 100

1. Fierce orange flames flew into the air.
2. The tin of yellow paint clattered to the floor.
3. I heard a crash and then everything went black.
4. The cute cat purred softly as I tickled its tummy.
5. A flock of colourful birds was chattering in the tree.
6. Our neighbour has just bought a sleek silver sports car.
7. A gruesome, grey, ghostly figure jumped out from behind the door.

Let's aim high now! page 100

2. The pink pig foraged for food. It grunted contentedly.
3. The silver snake slithered closer. It reared its head and hissed.
4. The dangerous brown dogs dashed towards us. They growled menacingly.
5. The great grey elephant lumbered across the road. It stopped, threw back its ears and trumpeted loudly.
6. The pretty purple parrot was perched on a pole. It squawked noisily at a passing crow.
7. The keen-eyed kookaburra spotted a green grasshopper. It chuckled gleefully.

Let's put it together now! page 101

The colours of nature

Nature **is** a jigsaw of different hues
Of the deepest greens and the softest **blues**
Nature's **like** a tapestry, woven with threads
Of beautiful browns and bright bold **reds**.
The colours of Nature stand happily together
Lavender next to grey; purple next to **silver**
They **threaten** us when thunder **roars** overhead
They soothe us in the evening when the sun goes to bed.

Let's have fun page 101

																1 c	r	e	a	m	
																r					
			2 g								3 i					i		4 o			
5 s	c	a	r	l	e	t					n					m		6 r	o	s	e
i			e				7 g				d					s		a			
8 l	a	v	e	n	d	e	r				i			9 b	r	o	w	n			
v			n				e				g			l		n		10 g	o	l	d
e							11 y	e	l	l	o	12 w		a				e			
13 r	e	d										h		c							
								14 b			15 p	i	n	k							
								l				t									
							16 p	u	r	p	l	e									
								e													

Let's have a test! page 102

1. From a distance, the Blue Mountains look like a dragon's back.
2. is as
3. She has a heart of gold.
4. are
5. load
6. The silver bell tinkled.
7. The big brown bear bounded towards us.
8. wild

Unit 18 Like and unlike

Let's find them! pages 103–104

1 lively **2** smooth **3** healthy **4** flexible
5 excellent **6** wide **7** manufactured

Let's go to the next step! page 104

1 scarce **2** compulsory **3** seldom **4** crooked
5 repulsive **6** dull **7** build

Let's aim high now! page 104

1 genuine **2** feeble **3** furious **4** praised
5 stubborn **6** abroad **7** misplaced

Let's find them! page 105

1 enjoyment **2** variety **3** interest **4** excitement
5 entertainment **6** information **7** value

Let's go to the next step! page 106

Verb/adjective	dom	ness	ment	ion
busy		business		
wise	**wisdom**			
enjoy			**enjoyment**	
explain				**explanation**
happy		**happiness**		
bore	**boredom**			
attract				**attraction**
announce			**announcement**	
create				**creation**
star	**stardom**			
punctuate				**punctuation**
pollute				**pollution**
forgive		**forgiveness**		
like		**likeness**		

Let's aim high now! page 106

1 enthusiasm **2** mildness, freshness
3 warmth, iciness **4** astonishment
5 kindness, cruelty **6** difference, confidence
7 willingness, unwillingness

Let's put it together now! page 107

Antonyms: different, spicy, savoury
Synonyms: scrumptious, friendly
Nouns: explosion, selection

Let's have fun page 107

b	x	t	v	s	t	y	l	y	a	c	f	j	m	l
e	e	a	g	h	d	k	l	n	e	i	e	a	s	y
a	o	m	p	r	l	q	u	a	s	s	x	b	e	g
u	y	e	k	l	o	p	d	m	s	y	z	d	h	h
t	a	m	x	f	y	g	w	j	x	a	i	p	f	g
y	c	n	e	i	p	l	d	w	q	m	g	x	h	i
j	g	k	f	r	e	e	d	o	m	z	j	k	r	h
p	l	n	f	n	v	c	s	g	h	s	t	a	l	e
r	n	o	k	l	s	x	b	h	a	x	w	t	h	m
e	r	i	i	e	s	s	e	n	i	l	g	u	b	c
c	q	s	t	s	v	z	x	t	u	i	a	q	f	s
i	u	i	u	r	h	s	j	v	g	n	o	r	t	s
o	y	v	f	t	n	e	b	h	s	q	t	u	g	c
u	z	e	g	w	y	i	x	q	s	j	j	a	d	r
s	z	r	k	y	w	a	m	u	s	e	m	e	n	t

Let's have a test! page 108

1 windy **2** sink, float **3** bold **4** eat, munch
5 Use multiplication, not division. **6** *ment*
7 softness **8** education

Notes

Notes

Notes